*PARTICIPATING:
PUBLIC SPEAKING, DEBATE,
AND DISCUSSION*

The Houghton Mifflin Communication Workshop

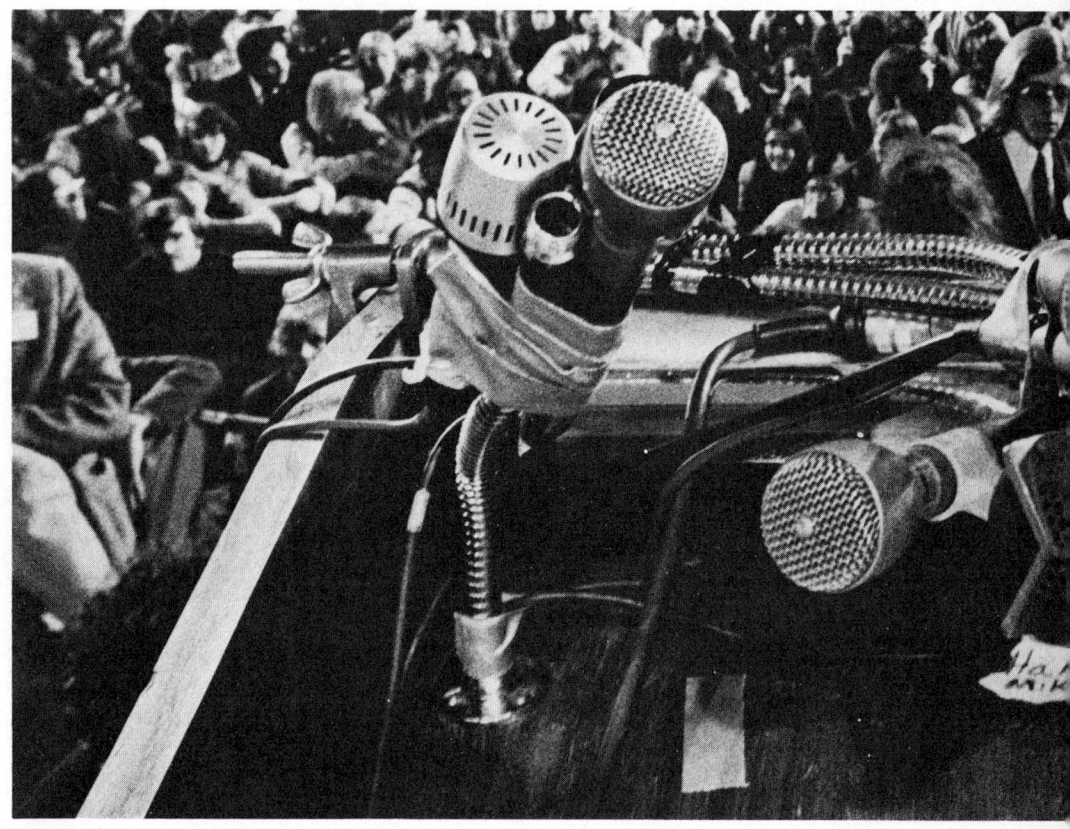

EDITORIAL ADVISER: Kathleen M. Galvin

Chairman, Speech Education Department
Northwestern University

Houghton Mifflin Company • Boston
Atlanta • Dallas • Geneva, Illinois • Hopewell, New Jersey • Palo Alto

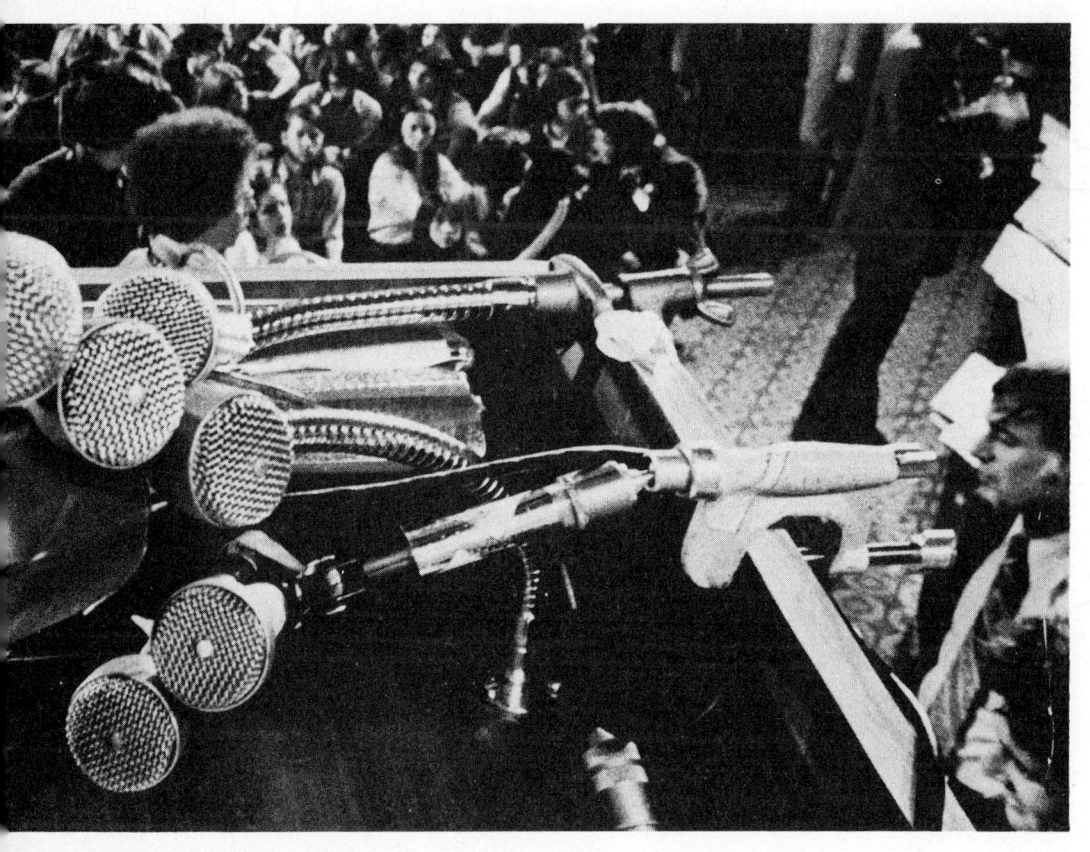

PARTICIPATING: PUBLIC SPEAKING, DEBATE, AND DISCUSSION

Ray G. Ewing

My special thanks to the following people for helping this book to come into being: Glenn L. Ewing, Faye Garten, and Lorene Ford for being model high school teachers and communicators; William D. Brooks for providing encouragement throughout the various stages of writing this book; Carolyn L. Ewing for typing the manuscript and for her insights and constructive feedback; Editorial Adviser Kathleen M. Galvin for suggestions helpful in completing this book.

—Ray G. Ewing

Dedicated to
Carolyn   Laura   Christina

Copyright © 1975 by Houghton Mifflin Company. All rights reserved. No part of this work may be reproduced or transmitted in any form or by any means, electronic or mechanical, including photocopying and recording, or by any information storage or retrieval system, without permission in writing from the publisher. Printed in the United States of America.

Library of Congress Catalog Card Number: 74-12844
ISBN: 0-395-19759-7

PHOTOGRAPHS AND ILLUSTRATIONS

Page x, Stephen Potter, Stock, Boston; p. 5, Jean-Claude Lejeune, Black Star; p. 9, Dan McCoy, Black Star; p. 12, Cradoc Bagshaw, Black Star; p. 14, Mike Mazzaschi, Stock, Boston; p. 18, Ira Kirschenbaum, Stock, Boston; p. 21, Ken Heyman; p. 22, Jerry Berndt, Boston; p. 26, Howard Bossen; p. 29, Susan Carlson; pp. 32-33, Ken Heyman; p. 38, Frank Siteman, Stock, Boston; p. 39, © King Features Syndicate 1973; p. 44, Cary Wolinsky, Stock, Boston; p. 50, Donald Dietz/Elizabeth Hamlin; p. 55, John T. Urban; p. 56, Tim Carlson, Stock, Boston; p. 58, John Rees, Black Star; Cary Wolinsky, Stock, Boston; Jack Prelutsky, Stock, Boston; Ken Heyman; p. 61, Tim Carlson, Stock, Boston; p. 63, Jeff Albertson, Stock, Boston; p. 68, New York Public Library; p. 71, Christopher S. Johnson, Stock, Boston; p. 75, Donald Wright Patterson, Jr., Stock, Boston; p. 78, The Bettman Archive; p. 80, Peter Hunsberger; p. 84, Daniel S. Brody, Stock, Boston; pp. 87, 92, Bob Fitch, Black Star; p. 96, Publishers-Hall Syndicate; p. 99, Donald Dietz/Elizabeth Hamlin; p. 104, Jon Goell; p. 106, Owen Franken, Stock, Boston; p. 112, Franklin Wing, Stock, Boston; p. 119, Patricia Hollander Gross, Stock, Boston; p. 121, Howard Bossen; p. 126, Russel Reif, Pictorial Parade; p. 132, Jon Goell; p. 135, Ellis Herwig, Stock, Boston; Ken Heyman; p. 139, Ginger Brown; p. 141, James Edward Vaughan, Black Star; p. 146, Ginger Brown; p. 148, NBC Photo; p. 151, Coca Cola Company; p. 155, Ken Heyman; p. 157, Ginger Brown; p. 160, John T. Urban, Stock, Boston; p. 164, Dan O'Neill, Editorial Photocolor Archives; p. 168, Bruce McAllister, Black Star; p. 171, Ira Kirschenbaum, Stock, Boston; p. 172, Owen Franken, Stock, Boston.

Cover created by Dorothy W. Moeller, using EPIC-II in collaboration with GTE Laboratories, Inc., Waltham, Mass. EPIC-II is one of the newest developments in the field of communication technology. It is an electronic device which enables an artist to change the shapes and colors of an image photographed by a TV camera and shown on a TV screen.

Title page photo: Jeff Albertson, Stock, Boston

Ballot on page 130 by permission of the American Forensic Association.

CONTENTS

From the Author   viii

SECTION ONE

1 CONCERNS FOR PUBLIC SPEAKING   1
How to get started

2 BUILDING A BELIEVABLE SPEECH   15
How to develop your ideas

3 ORGANIZING AND EXPRESSING   27
How to use thoughts and words

4 BRINGING IT ALL TOGETHER   45
How to deliver your speech

5 AUDIENCE FEEDBACK   59
How to use it and give it

SECTION TWO

6 THE CHALLENGE OF PLEASANT DISAGREEMENT   69
How to write a debate proposition for classroom use

7 GETTING AT THE ISSUES 81
How to analyze debate propositions

8 GETTING YOUR IDEAS TOGETHER 93
How to build sound arguments

9 THE DEBATE ITSELF 113
How to present your point of view

SECTION THREE

10 WE'RE IN THIS THING TOGETHER 133
How groups work

11 THERE ARE NO SMALL PARTS,
ONLY SMALL ACTORS 149
How to take part in a discussion

12 WHO'S IN CHARGE AROUND HERE? 161
How to chair a discussion group

Books to Read 174

Glossary of Terms 177

Index 179

From the author . . .

I wish I could talk with you instead of writing to you. Talking with you would give me a chance to prepare my remarks just for you. It would also give me a chance to adjust my remarks to your smiles, your frowns, and your questions. You could take another side of an issue or together we could discuss ways of solving certain problems. My talking with you would also help you better understand my ideas.

The increased understanding that can result from speaking about topics in public, or publicly debating or discussing ideas, is one of the reasons that people in our society spend so much of their time participating in public communication.

Of course this increased understanding isn't automatic -- you don't play a musical instrument perfectly the first time you try. Increased understanding -- and with it an improved society -- only comes about as people learn to talk and listen well.

You noticed that I said learn to talk and listen well.

Some people are obviously better public speakers, debaters, or discussion participants than others. Why? Because they know more about the principles of public communication and have spent more time practicing the needed skills.

I trust that you'll develop into a better participant as you go through this book. Then, your understanding -- and society's -- will increase!

That's my hope!

Ray G. Ewing

Section 1

Concerns For Public Speaking 1

How to get started

Your world is seldom silent. You fill the air with shouts, questions, and whispered thoughts. The world in turn bombards you with messages that cry out for a response from you. As you walk out the door to school your mother shouts to you, "Get your hair out of your eyes!" Two younger friends playing kick ball get into an argument and ask you to settle it.

THE NEED TO SPEAK WITH OTHERS

The above situations will probably require only a private conversation between you and a few other people. However, suppose a friend at school invites you to campaign for her at the assembly to nominate student officers. What if friends ask you to get up and voice their concerns about poor library policies or a weak intramural program? You may be asked by a teacher to give a speech to entertain in order to reduce tensions or build school morale. In these situations the *needs and tensions of others create the need for you to speak up in public.*

Your own needs and tensions can do the same. If you're upset that letter jackets are awarded to boys but not to girls or that there are twice as many male counselors as female, you can probably find opportunities to voice your views. If you want to become a doctor but your school lacks a quality science program, or if you merely want to shoot a few baskets after school but the school grounds are locked tight at four, you can speak up as a result of your own felt needs.

CHOOSING A TOPIC FOR CLASS

Most of the time in class, however, you'll probably be making speeches—or participating in debates or discussions—because you've been given an assignment. The teacher asks you to prepare a five-minute speech for Friday and your immediate response is "But what will I talk about?"

When you choose a topic for a speech, the best place to begin is with yourself. Have you had any experiences that would amuse or help others in class? Do you know something about a subject that would be interesting to others?

You may protest that you're not an authority on anything. Well, no one knows all there is to know about anything. If you know enough about something to be interested in it, then it shouldn't be too hard for you to develop that topic into a speech. If you're really interested in your topic, you're well on your way to giving a good speech.

To help you focus on your interests, you might take a sheet of paper and fill out your own speech topic finder.

Speech Topic Finder

☐ Copy these headings and fill in as many of your interests and likes as you can think of.

Books	Entertainers	Hobbies
Jobs	Movies	Politicians
School Subjects	Sports	TV Shows

Add as many categories as you like!

☐ To discover more about yourself and to help yourself focus on possible topics, keep a diary of potential topics for speeches for one week. Do this by clipping out articles that you read in the paper and by keeping notes on shows that you watch and things that you do. Examine your diary of topics at the end of one week. Do your interests fit into most of the categories you already have on your topic finder, or will you create new categories?

SPEECH PURPOSES

Once you've decided on a particular topic, you must then decide on what you want to accomplish when speaking on that topic. Do you want people to be amused and entertained? Do you want them to know more about the topic than they did before? Do you want them to believe as you do or act as you do?

What you want to accomplish may be referred to as your speech *purpose*. According to one theory all speeches have a persuasive purpose—to cause others to respond in whatever way the speaker wishes. Another theory lists three general purposes of speech: (1) to entertain, (2) to inform, and (3) to persuade.

You give a speech to *entertain* in order to share a few moments of enjoyment with your audience. You give a speech to *inform* in order to increase the understanding of listeners about some particular topic. You give a speech to *persuade* in order to get others to agree with your beliefs or to take some action.

☐ Read the topics in the following list and think about them for a moment. Then, in three columns, indicate which of the topics you would choose for a speech to entertain, which for a speech to inform, and which for a speech to persuade.
1. Watching TV commercials
2. Using the term Ms.
3. The rating system for movies
4. Auto racing
5. Girls and boys playing on the same athletic teams
6. Requiring a foreign language for high school graduation

7. Careers in medicine
8. High school marriages
9. Compulsory school attendance
10. Telling white lies

☐ Compare your list with the lists prepared by your classmates. Are there differences of opinion? Can some of the topics be used for entertaining *and* informing *and* persuading? If so, which ones and why?

When you discussed your answers with your classmates, you probably did discover some differences of opinion. That leads us to another important point: in preparing a speech, you must consider not only your own interests and purpose, but also those of your audience.

"GETTING WITH" AN AUDIENCE

Suppose you've just moved, and are starting out in a new school. How do you become friends with your new classmates? Probably by learning something about them. What do they like to talk about? Do they like people who show a sense of humor or are they "serious" most of the time? What are their interests? Their backgrounds?

Or suppose you've decided to apply to college but find you have to raise your grade average. You'll probably do some extra studying, but you may also try to analyze your teachers to find out what else you might do to raise your grades. Do your teachers appreciate questions in class, or do they frown on them? Do they encourage students to express various points of view, or do they prefer that students listen quietly in class? What kinds of behavior and answers are considered strictly taboo?

Whether your goal is trying to entertain others, to give them information, or to persuade them of something, the need for understanding your audience stays the same. As a new student doffs boots for sandals after noticing that no one else wears boots, or an infielder shifts for a left-handed pull hitter, so a public speaker adjusts to audience needs and interests in order to achieve positive results.

DEMOGRAPHIC CHARACTERISTICS

The more you can find out about audience members the better you can prepare your speech for them. Information about certain *demographic factors* may provide important clues about an audience. (Demographic factors include age, nationality, race, religion, and sex.)

More than 2,000 years ago, the Greek philosopher Aristotle wrote of the differences in character between young and old people. You can no doubt think of many exceptions to his generalizations; there are "young" grandmothers and "old" teenagers. Still, it is interesting to look at the differences Aristotle observed.

Character of Young Men	*Character of Elderly Men*
Changeable; emotional	Self-controlled
Love honor and victory over others	Love for life
Not very impressed by money	Learned to value money
Optimistic	Cynical
Looking to the future	Live more by memory
Value noble deeds, idealistic	Practical
Enjoy friends and companions	Value others for usefulness
Tendency to do things in excess	Tendency to "under do"

If you accept the idea that there are some basic differences between young people and older people, then you will emphasize different things when talking with different age groups. For example, when speaking with younger audiences, a candidate for office might stress the need for commitment to the "highest of ideals" so that all people might live in a better world, thus appealing to the idealism of most young people. The same candidate speaking with an older audience might appeal to the older people's practicality. He would tend to place more emphasis upon his past accomplishments, and to explain how he intends "to get the job done" if elected. In both situations, the candidate would use examples to illustrate that he understands the needs and life styles of most members of his particular audience.

☐ Work in small groups of three or four people. Discuss whether or not you think Aristotle's lists are accurate.
Can you name young people who fit Aristotle's "young" list? His "old" list?

☐ Aristotle, of course, lived long before the days of the women's liberation movement. Do you think his lists could apply to women as well as men? Why, or why not?

☐ Make up your own "young" and "old" lists.

☐ Assume that together you are going to prepare a speech for a group of:
   a. middle-aged school librarians
   b. teenaged girls
   c. Cub Scouts
   d. middle-aged business people

Your topic is "Leisure Time Activities."

☐ Keeping in mind qualities from Aristotle's "young/old" list, or your own, list the kinds of activities each group would enjoy hearing about. What special advantages would appeal to each group the most?

☐ Compare your answers with those of other groups.

Cultural differences

Cultural differences call for differences in word choices and attitude. Any speaker trying to communicate effectively with audience members should study their life styles and language habits in order to be clearly understood and avoid offending anyone. For example, if you're talking to a group of adult Americans of German descent and you mention *sauerbraten*, they'll probably know what you mean. But if your audience is a sixth-grade class in an area in which most people's grandparents came from Spain, they probably won't be familiar with the term.

Far more serious, however, is the danger of accidentally offending an audience because you don't know enough about them or haven't thought about what your words might sound like from their point of view. Certain attitudes and uses of language are almost guaranteed to produce ill-will even though the speaker has the best of intentions. To avoid negative responses you should try to avoid statements that tend to (1) stereotype, (2) patronize, or (3) over-identify.

Stereotyping

The speaker who tends to ignore individual differences among members of any group may encounter resentment even when he or she thinks his or her comments are positive. Not *all* black people have rhythm, or good voices, or soul. Sam may appreciate a *personal* compliment, but not the statement, "Man, all you guys can sure sing!" People resent even more remarks that stereotype negatively. Such comments as: "Mexicans are lazy; Indians are undependable; WASPS are greedy materialists," reveal a lack of understanding and experience on the part of the speaker.

Patronizing

Patronizing statements are those that sound as if a speaker feels superior to his or her listeners. Such statements are almost certain to produce negative responses. You've heard such patronizing remarks as "I remember I used to feel that way when I was your age, but now I ..." or "We've worked hard to get where we are now and you have the same opportunities so be patient, work hard, and...." Such remarks indicate the speaker feels he or she has everything to give to and nothing to gain from the audience. A speaker should *talk with* audience members in such a way that all may benefit from the experience.

OVER-IDENTIFICATION

While identification with audience members—emphasizing things you have in common—is a key to acceptance, over-identification may prevent acceptance. For me to tell a group of Sioux or Cherokee that "I'm part Indian myself" will likely be viewed as an obvious attempt at identification. The statement may be true, but how much has my "part Indian" known of the needs and struggles of the people I'm talking with? Too often speakers try to substitute superficial signs and relationships for a lack of shared experiences. To adopt another person's style of clothing, hair, or music is not necessarily to touch that person's being. To glibly assert such understanding is to invite harsh rebuttal.

The religious beliefs of others will also affect the speaker's choice of topic and style of presentation. Certain subjects would be inappropriate for certain groups of people. For instance, a speech advocating "Military Preparedness" would not be appropriate for an audience of Quakers.

Audiences with certain attitudes or religious persuasions may automatically reject a speaker who uses certain words or expressions they consider vulgar. Other audiences may accept a limited number of such words as necessary for emphasis. You need to be true to your own convictions, but also remember that you must not deliberately offend your audience.

Until recently, many speakers felt a need for different approaches to male and female audiences. Now, however, women are increasingly involved in politics, business, sports, and other aspects of life once considered strictly male activities—and increasing numbers of men are moving into "female" careers like elementary teaching and secretarial work. So your approach to a topic should depend more on what you know about your listeners as individuals rather than on the fact that you're speaking to nine men and twenty women. If your audience is all male or all female, be careful of assuming that all the men are football fans or that all the women are skilled cooks—unless you know that for a fact.

In preparing a speech, you need to know more about audience members than demographic facts: age, nationality, race, religion, and sex. You need to know the answers to three important questions about audience members. (1) What are their attitudes toward the topic of the speech? (2) How much do they know about the topic? (3) What are their attitudes toward the speaker?

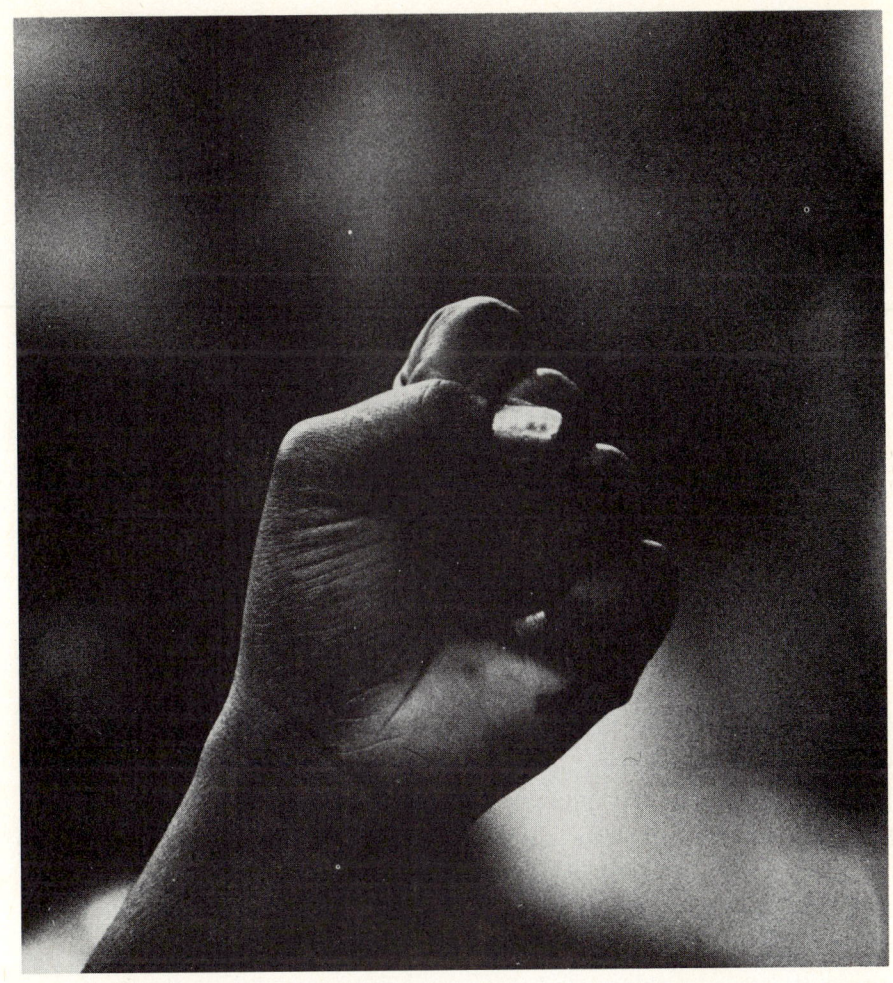

Attitudes Toward Topic

The common bonds and feelings that bring people together can tell you more about preparing a particular speech than "census-type" data. The bonds that unite sports-car buffs or lovers of bluegrass music may be stronger than obvious distinctions based on age or race. If audience members have great interest in a given topic, their attention does not need to be won—only kept.

However, an audience that gathers out of casual curiosity or compulsion needs careful cultivation. Students in a classroom are usually there by compulsion, not by choice. In that situation you might begin with an illustration or example designed to dramatize the importance of the topic to class members. Humor and colorful examples can also help win and hold an audience's interest.

Joe Garagiola, in explaining some of the strategy behind his TV show, *The Baseball World of Joe Garagiola,* stated that he aims for the marginal fan since the dedicated fan will watch anyway. Garagiola has presented shows dealing with such diverse topics as songs about baseball, poetry about baseball, and the production and distribution of baseball cards. Similarly, you could well expect Shakespearean scholars to be interested in almost any topic related to Shakespeare. You might not reach non-scholars unless you talked about something with more "human" appeal—like how to costume a Shakespearean play, or how "special effects" were handled at the Globe Theater in sixteenth-century England.

Occasionally you may be confronted by an audience that is hostile. What do you do when most students want to make a class contribution to improve the athletic field, but you want to convince them to buy books for the library? What do you do when most people are satisfied to go along with the way things are out of fear of "rocking the boat," but you're incensed that citizens don't demand more responsible leadership? In such situations you have to demonstrate your understanding of others' points of view and acknowledge that they have some good reasons for their position. If all you do is attack their position, you'll probably only intensify their opposition. There is a great deal of truth in the old adage "You can catch more flies with honey than with vinegar." No one likes to be told his or her viewpoint is immoral or unreasonable or stupid. If you wish to have your viewpoint considered, give the opposition credit for caring about the problem, and show some way in which your beliefs can benefit them. Present the many sides of the basic issue, but give final emphasis to the advantages of your position.

It's very easy to presume that you and other students in class are alike in everything—simply because you know you like the same kinds of music. Listening to the same records and wearing the same hair styles won't guarantee that others will vote as you do in student elections. Similarly, if you feel outside the "in group" you may exaggerate the differences between yourself and other students. You may think they're not interested in hearing about life on the farm because they've grown up in the city. Well, you may be surprised. So, even though you think you know what your classmates are like, try to find out more about them.

Prior Knowledge about Topic

How well your audience already understands your topic will also influence your speaking strategies. Relatively uninformed listeners will need to hear more background information and more clarifying examples than will listeners who already know a lot. For such an uninformed audience you may also have to use more strategies designed to maintain attention: visual aids, more humor, suspense-building techniques, or livelier delivery (see Chapter 4).

Don't assume, however, that an informed audience won't need such attention-focusing strategies. The need is there—it just isn't as great. Informed audience members don't need a lengthy presentation of materials they already understand, but they do appreciate an interesting presentation, and a comparison of what they know with new bits of information.

Time Limitations

The restrictions of time and place also put limits on ideas and examples. It is difficult to explain the background of all the problems in the Middle East and offer ways to solve them in a five-minute speech. You'll usually be given a time limit when you're asked to make a speech. If not, ask how long you have. Then you can focus your speech so the subject is manageable within the time allotted. Keep your purpose—*and your audience*—in mind when you do this.

SUMMING UP

Your own needs or those of others will often cause you to speak up in public. In the classroom your reason for speaking in front of the class is usually an assignment. Picking a topic for that assignment involves choosing something of interest to you and to your audience. In making that topic more specific you must decide on your purpose and the limits you must place on your topic because of time restrictions.

The next—and most vital—step in preparing your speech is to analyze your audience. What kinds of people are in your audience? How old are they? What religion? Race? Nationality? Sex? What do they know about your topic? What are their attitudes toward it? Once you have some answers to these vital questions you are ready to consider their attitudes toward you, and you are ready to begin *building a believable speech*.

Activities

☐   Choose a topic on which to write a speech. The list on pages 3–4 may give you some ideas. Now, write down all the facts you think your classmates will know on that topic. Then write what you think might be their attitudes on the topic.

☐   Work in small groups of four or five. Take five to ten minutes to interview others in your group to find out what they know and how they feel about your topic.

☐   Compare the answers you received from your classmates in the second activity with the answers you wrote down in the first activity. Are there any major differences? Will you change your topic? Your purpose? Your preparation? Why?

☐   In small groups, discuss why and how an Indian speaking on Indian Rights might change his or her specific purpose or approach when speaking to:
    a. The Lions Club
    b. Members of the Black Cultural Center
    c. The League of Women Voters
    d. Your class

☐   Have the different groups compare answers. Discuss any major differences of opinion.

Building A Believable Speech   2

How to develop your ideas

Much of your willingness to listen to someone else is based on the way you feel about the person talking with you. If you have positive feelings about someone, you tend to believe him or her even in the face of strong statements to the contrary. If a fight breaks out at school and your best friend tells you how it happened, you will tend to believe him or her even if you hear six other versions of the incident. Because of certain past experiences, your friend is believable, or credible.

A speaker the audience already knows and likes obviously has an easier task than a speaker the audience doesn't know or like. If your audience doesn't know you, you have to work to establish yourself as worthy of trust. You must demonstrate that you know what you are talking about, that you are credible, and that you have the best interests of your audience at heart. You can best demonstrate these positive factors by careful advance preparation of the speech. This advance preparation involves (1) knowing your subject well, (2) selecting supportive materials, (3) organizing ideas and materials effectively, and (4) choosing the "best" words to be used with the particular audience. This chapter will discuss the first two items.

Knowing Your Subject Well

As suggested in the first chapter, start with a topic you're interested in and know something about. But don't stop with what you already know. Expand your interest and knowledge by interviewing others who share your interests, particularly if you view them as greater authorities than you are. Make use of your school and community libraries. Use the card catalogue and the *Readers' Guide to Periodical Literature* to trace down sources that can refine your thinking and clarify your ideas in a speech. For subjects currently of interest, read articles in your daily newspaper and weekly news magazines and be alert for television news specials. In searching for information, don't limit yourself to information that supports your point of view. Gather information about the many sides of your particular subject. This may lead to an unexpected change of viewpoint on your part, but that's one of the exciting things about research. Whether your original point of view changes or not, you will be better prepared to talk with others if you understand your subject from more than one point of view.*

☐ Pick one of the following controversial topics:
1. Outlawing the manufacture and sale of handguns
2. Repealing all censorship laws and controls
3. Legalizing gambling in all states
4. Federal support of private schools
5. _____ (Your choice)

☐ Write a short paragraph stating your point of view about the topic you have chosen.

☐ Then research an opposing view by finding newspaper and magazine articles about it. Write a short paragraph stating the opposing viewpoint that you've read about.

---

* For more about research, see *Investigating: Gathering Information,* by Jane Stine, in this series.

☐   Has your point of view changed? If so, how? What was it in the opposing view that changed your thinking? If your point of view hasn't changed, why hasn't it? What do you disagree with most about the opposing viewpoint? Why?

As you delve into other materials, it is important to take accurate notes that will be helpful in building your speech. Most experienced speakers record information on note cards. They are careful to *title* the card according to the *central idea* or fact recorded, and to include the *author,* the printed *source, date,* and *page* number(s).* It is also wise to find and jot down information about any expert you may quote. Your quoting Clarence Kelley means more to your audience if you can point out to them that he's a former Kansas City police chief and FBI director. (Information about many living authorities may be discovered in such publications as *Who's Who in America* and *Current Biography. The Dictionary of American Biography* contains information about deceased Americans of great prominence, while most encyclopedias have articles about prominent people living and dead.)

RESPONSIBLE SPEAKING

Are your ideas important to you? Would you be upset if someone passed off an idea of yours as his or her own? You would, very likely. So, when you are preparing a speech, be very careful about using the thoughts of other people. It's certainly all right to use them—just be *sure* you give credit where it's due. Passing off another person's words, thoughts, or ideas as your own—deliberately or accidentally—is plagiarism. It is a kind of theft, even if you don't quote exactly.

It is also important that you record information accurately and report it clearly so that its meaning is not distorted. Leaving out a "not," "seldom," or "never" can quickly change the meaning of a quotation. If the principal said that "Rachel seldom gets into trouble" and you report him or her as saying "Rachel gets into trouble" you've obviously distorted the

---

* Again, see *Investigating: Gathering Information,* by Jane Stine, the chapters on note-taking and organizing material.

meaning. Leaving the zero off a number—changing the reported storm damage from $1,000 to $100—also distorts. So, be sure to copy information accurately.

Selecting Supportive Materials

In selecting and developing materials for use in a speech it is important to remember that their main function is to make your purpose clearer and more acceptable to your audience. People don't laugh if they don't understand the punch line. Students can't learn if ideas aren't clearly explained. Audience members won't be persuaded to "take up the cause" if your "proof" is not acceptable to them.

Merely stating an idea and mentioning some authority or showing a vague statistical chart does not guarantee that others will accept the idea as "proven." Proving an idea literally means making it acceptable to your audience. Your supportive materials should be chosen on the basis of the amount of faith your audience will put in them.

Types of Supportive Materials

There are five main types of materials used to clarify or support ideas. They are *examples, visual aids, testimony, comparisons,* and *statistics.*

Examples If you are preparing a brief speech on "Some Endangered Species and How They Might Be Saved" you would almost certainly wish to use two or three examples. But, in order to make your point, it would not be necessary to list every endangered mammal or fowl.

A speaker may choose to use a more *expanded example* to illustrate a point. In demonstrating that traditional attitudes toward summer school may be on the way out, a speaker might point to the following as an *expanded example* of changing attitudes:

Some Chicago schools are now in operation year-round on a 45-15 plan. Students attend classes for 45 consecutive weekdays, and then take the next 15 weekdays off. Students and faculty are divided into four groups, with three groups in school and one group on vacation at all times. Students are assigned their 45-15 schedules by neighborhood, so that students from the same family will attend school together and will have friends nearby when they are on vacation.

Hypothetical — or "what if," examples may be used to stimulate audience members to act: "If you were threatened by a thief, what would you do?" Such examples usually appeal to the basic physical and psychological needs common to us all. We don't like situations that threaten us with loss of life, physical well-being, freedom, or self-esteem. Most people therefore support ideas that promise physical well-being, improved relationships with others, or greater opportunities for self-development.

☐ Write down supportive materials for a speech on "The Mistreatment of Minorities by the Majority in the United States."
   a. List three specific examples you might use.
   b. Develop one expanded example.
   c. Create one hypothetical example.

☐ Compare answers in class. Does any one kind of example seem to be more effective than the others?

☐ Write down supportive materials for a speech on "The Mistreatment of the Majority by the Minority."
   a. List three specific examples you might use.
   b. Develop one expanded example.
   c. Create one hypothetical example.

☐ Were these examples easier or harder to think of than those in the first activity? Why? Which speech would be the easiest to support and deliver in your class? Why?

Visual aids can be particularly effective in clarifying ideas and making them memorable. A speech about "The Destructive Force of a Tornado" will be more interesting if the speaker uses charts showing weather conditions that contribute to the formation of tornadoes and photographs of the damage tornadoes have caused.

In using visual aids there are a few "do's" and "don'ts" that you should remember. 1. *Do* check the room and equipment in advance. If you are going to use posters or charts, check for a stand to put them on or clasps by which you can suspend them. Holding a poster for any length of time is awkward, and attempting to stand it on the chalk rail of a blackboard is relaxing for the poster but not for the speaker. Make sure electrical outlets are available in convenient locations if you intend to use records, slides, or film. Always check your equipment "on location" to make sure no needle has been broken in transit, no bulb has burned out, and no film has been wound backwards.

2. *Do* make sure that your aids will be easily seen by everyone. Posters should be large enough to be seen by those in the back row. Letters or graph lines must be dark and bold enough to be easily read. If you use objects or models, be sure that each detail you are going to point out and discuss will be visible to the audience.

3. *Don't* block the view of audience members. When you call attention to a particular part of a drawing, stand to one side of it and point with the hand closest to it so you don't turn your body away from the audience. Audience members whose views are blocked by the speaker, or by poor placement of a visual aid, tend to lose interest fast!

4. *Don't* pass materials around during a speech. The postcards, stamps, or Mexican jumping beans will become the focus of attention—and you will soon find you are talking to yourself instead of with your audience.

Testimony is a statement, quoted by a speaker, showing that *someone else*—usually an expert—agrees with the point the speaker is trying to make.

In seeking approval of an idea by using testimony, it is important to use a source who is actually an authority in the field you are discussing. A baseball player may be a marvel on the diamond, but that won't necessarily make him a nutritional expert. There is no need, therefore, to change our breakfast eating habits on a shortstop's advice.

Quoted authorities should be known authorities. We are more apt to accept the views of someone whose name we recognize as an authority. If you want to quote Professor G. Rupert Goatbeard but you know your audience hasn't heard of him, you have two choices. You can use a better known authority. Or, you can tell your audience why Professor Goatbeard is an authority before you actually quote him.

Quoted sources should also be sources your audience will respect. Members of the Democratic party aren't likely to applaud a speaker quoting extensively from Republicans like Barry Goldwater or William F. Buckley. Likewise, conservative Republicans aren't going to sign many petitions for a speaker quoting extensively from liberals like George McGovern or Tom Wicker. Some people read *U.S. News & World Report*, while others subscribe to *Newsweek*. You must know which sources are most respected by your audience in order to use testimony effectively.

Comparisons may be used to clarify one concept by pointing out its similarities and differences in relation to another concept. A Chevrolet salesman will attempt to sell his car by pointing out features that it has that a Ford does not. In seeking to gain new members for a club, a club member might contrast the advantages of membership with the disadvantages of not belonging to the organization.

Of course, a speaker needs to be fair and complete when making comparisons. For example, club membership may help you win new friends and increased recognition, but it would also impose new demands on your time and finances. A good speaker doesn't lie and say there are no disadvantages in membership. Instead, he or she points out how the advantages outweigh any disadvantages.

Statistics are bits of information presented in numerical form. Some people seem to worship computer print-outs and doubt the truth of any observations which have not been measured and tabulated. Others seem unimpressed by figures, particularly when the figures aren't in line with their real life experiences. The decision to use statistics should depend on whether or not your audience respects them.

You should observe certain precautions in order to use statistics fairly and effectively. Check all figures to make sure they are accurate and up-to-date. Stock market figures, for example, indicate the value of particular stocks on a given day: the figures change daily. Most statistics must be viewed as a reflection of *particular conditions at a particular time.*

If you seek to support an idea by citing the results of a poll, be sure the sampling is sufficiently large and representative. If the students in your school were polled to find out how they felt about the spending of funds for the coming school year, the poll probably wouldn't reflect student opinion very accurately if only five students were questioned. It would be even less fair if all five were members of a particular group—the band or the industrial arts club.

Someone once stated that figures don't lie, but liars do figure. Poll results are not worth using when questions are obviously loaded. What does it mean to say that 95% of the citizens of your community favor "law and order"? Does it mean they favor gun control? Outlawing strikes and boycotts? Tougher penalties for crime? It's difficult to know. It's also difficult to answer "no" to a question like "Do you favor law and order?" A "no" answer seems to say you support crime. The question is so loaded as to make results meaningless.

SUMMING UP

Building a believable speech involves knowing as much as you can about your subject, and selecting supportive materials most likely to be accepted by your audience. Your search for materials can lead you to a variety of sources. Your responsibility then is to record those sources accurately and give them proper credit in your speech.

The five main types of materials used to clarify and support ideas are *examples, visual aids, testimony, comparisons,* and *statistics.* It is important that you check out these materials to see how supportive they really are—and how likely your audience will be to accept them.

Activities

☐ You are asked to give a speech to your class on "Some Ways High School Students Can Earn Money."
    List three sources that you might go to for information.
    List five specific supportive materials you might use—one
       of each type mentioned in this chapter.

☐ You want to talk your parents into letting you take a particular job—you pick the job. How will you go about convincing them that you should take the job to earn some money?
    List three sources that you might go to for information.
    List five specific supportive materials you might use—one
       of each type mentioned in this chapter.

☐ Would you go to the same sources for material for both of the speeches above? Why, or why not?

☐ Would you use the same supportive materials for both speeches? Why, or why not? Would one type of supportive material be more effective with one audience than with the other? Explain.

Organizing And Expressing 3

How to use thoughts and words

You read this book by moving your eyes from left to right, beginning at the upper left hand corner of a page and concluding at the lower right hand corner, following a pattern. Weather is predicted on the basis of patterns in warm and cold fronts, barometric pressure, and so forth. Jobs are made easier and quicker when you develop patterns for completing them. Discovering patterns, in short, seems to make things easier to understand.

Audience members are more likely to understand and remember a speaker's ideas if the ideas are organized in an easily perceived pattern. Listeners don't have anything on paper to see how ideas are organized. Neither do they have the chance—as they do with written material—to go over again something that they don't understand. This fact about oral communication makes it imperative that your ideas be easily understood the first time—it may be the only time!

In planning a trip, whether it be to a department store blocks away or to a city hundreds of miles away, you map out a route that will be the quickest, or the safest, or the most scenic. So it is that in a particular speech you must map out an approach with particular objectives in mind. If you don't map out your trip—or speech—carefully, the results may be disastrous!

ORGANIZING YOUR THOUGHTS

Traditionally speeches have been divided into three basic parts: (1) Introduction, (2) Body, and (3) Conclusion. We're going to start with the body of the speech, however, since there is no need to develop an introduction until there is something to introduce. Some of the basic patterns used to organize the major points of the body of a speech are the *chronological pattern, spatial pattern, topical pattern, problem-solution pattern, deductive pattern, inductive pattern,* and *psychological pattern.*

The **chronological pattern** is used when the elements of a speech demand a particular order because of a necessary time sequence. If you are explaining how to defuse a bomb, it's crucial to your listeners that you explain it step by step. If you're telling how to make a cake, it's important to say that certain ingredients must be added before others: frosting ingredients are not added to the batter. If you are describing a camping trip or political campaign, outlining it and then telling about it *in sequence* will help the audience understand and remember it.

Spatial Pattern A description of a vacation trip from Lafayette, Indiana, to Toronto, Canada, tends to follow both a chronological pattern and a *spatial pattern.* You might describe what you did at each major stop on the trip—going from Lafayette to Fort Wayne, to Detroit, to London, Ontario, and finally to Toronto! A spatial pattern might also be used in explaining the operation of a particular factory where a friend of yours may work. You could explain the different functions of equipment in various areas of the factory. In that situation too, space is the element which relates each point to all other main points.

A **topical pattern** may be used when a subject seems to fall naturally into particular categories. For instance, a speech about women in political life might be arranged as follows:
- I. Women Elected as Governmental Officials
    - A. Representative Barbara Jordan
    - B. Representative Margaret Heckler
    - C. Representative Elizabeth Holtzman
- II. Women Involved in the Civil Rights Movement
    - A. Shirley Chisholm
    - B. Coretta King
    - C. LaDonna Harris

   III. Women Involved in Various Other Political Activities
      A. Lady Bird Johnson
      B. Gloria Steinem
      C. Shirley MacLaine

    The **problem-solution pattern** is the one usually used by debate teams. The problem, or need, is presented first. After convincing people that the problem exists, you present your proposed solution, or plan. Then you demonstrate how that plan will solve the problem. An example of the three points used in such a pattern follows:

    Problem: Lack of money for a class field trip.

    Proposed Solution: Hold a car wash in the school parking lot a week from Saturday.

    Plan Solves Problem: A car wash raised over $250 for Tech High seniors last year. We need to raise only $200 to go on the trip. Therefore, the car wash should solve our problem.

The **deductive** and **inductive patterns** come from the two basic forms of reasoning, *deduction* and *induction*. Deduction begins with a generally held truth, called a *major premise,* and arrives, often via a specific instance, called a *minor premise,* at a *conclusion* about a particular person or principle.

Deductive reasoning makes use of a formalized three-step pattern known as a syllogism. An example of such reasoning would be:

Major Premise: All debate coaches have college degrees.
(generally held truth)
Minor Premise: Ms. Reffett is a debate coach.
(specific instance or application)
Conclusion: Therefore, Ms. Reffett has a college degree.

The above conclusion is correct providing (1) the major premise is true—with no exceptions, and (2) the subject of the minor premise (Ms. Reffett) properly belongs in the general class (debate coaches) referred to in the major premise. You might remember this another way: If either the major premise or minor premise is false, the conclusion will be false.

Another rule to remember about syllogisms is that if both premises are negative, no conclusion can be reached.

Major Premise: No science teachers coach debate.
Minor Premise: Mr. Crisson is not a science teacher.
Conclusion: Therefore, Mr. Crisson _____.

No conclusion can be reached. You may speculate as to whether or not Mr. Crisson is a debate coach, but an answer cannot possibly be deduced from the premises.

If you use the **deductive pattern** in a speech, then you begin by stating a generalization that is already accepted by your listeners. Then you show that specific instances relate to the accepted generalization and thus lead logically to the specific conclusion.

Accepted Generalization: Dishonest politicians should be removed from office.
Specific Instances: In Instances A, B, C, and D, Politician X has used the power of public office to increase his own power and wealth.
Specific Conclusion: Politician X should be removed from office.

Inductive reasoning is the reverse of deductive reasoning. It starts with specific facts or instances and builds from them to a general statement or principle. This line of reasoning is actually the way we build most of the assumptions we live by. Some logicians claim that all reasoning is ultimately inductive.

Scientists observe certain things happening—for example, chickens seem to lay more eggs when the chicken house is at a certain temperature. From these observations scientists set up a general statement: "Air temperature affects egg production." This general statement, called a *hypothesis,* is then tested. To be proved true, it must be tested by more frequent and more controlled observations.

In everyday life, people sometimes try to motivate others to reason inductively in order to solve particular problems or to avoid a confrontation. For example, your little brother might mention to your parents that Laura and Tom are going to camp this summer. Later he lets them know that Derek and Dean are also going—and Lisa and Sandy, too. Your parents may then reason inductively that his entire class is going to camp —and that he wants to go too.

If you use the *inductive pattern* in a speech, you give the audience specific examples and then move to a conclusion dictated by those examples.

Example 1: Former school debater Earl Hunsaker is now President of the Student Senate at State U.

Example 2: Former school debater Dorothy Meredith is now a State Representative.

Example 3: Former school debater Louis Hawker is now serving as our district attorney.

Conclusion, or inference drawn: High school debate helps prepare students for positions of leadership and responsibility in our society.

☐ Turn the example using Politican X into an inductive pattern.

☐ Turn the example stressing the importance of high school debate into a deductive pattern.

☐ Which pattern—deductive or inductive—would be the best to use with an audience hostile to your viewpoint? Why?

A **psychological pattern** of organization is one designed to obtain certain psychological responses from the listener. A well-known psychological pattern was designed by Alan Monroe, former professor at Purdue University. This pattern, referred to as *Monroe's Motivated Sequence,* has five basic steps.

Steps	Function
1. Attention	To gain audience's attention.
2. Need	To create a need to know (informative speech) or need to change (persuasive speech).
3. Satisfaction	To present information or plan that will satisfy the need created in step 2.
4. Visualization	To get audience to visualize what will happen if plan is not adopted and/or what could happen if it is.
5. Action	To get audience members to commit themselves to a specific course of action.

In some cases, you will not need to use all five steps in the Sequence. For example, if your purpose is to entertain or to inform your audience, you may need to consider only the first three steps. But if your purpose is to persuade, you will need all five.

☐ Develop a brief outline, using *Monroe's Motivated Sequence,* that deals with a large problem such as improving our environment. Label each of the five steps.

☐ You might begin work on the outline by seeking to provide answers to these questions:

Attention	What can you say or do to focus student attention on environmental problems?
Need	What can you say or do to show that these problems really affect the people of your community—the students in your class? (Maybe use some visual aids? If so, describe them.)
Satisfaction	What information or plan can you present that will help solve local environmental problems?
Visualization	Can you describe what things would be like if everyone pitched in? What if they didn't?
Action	Is there a local organization students can join in order to help out? Could your class really do something to help?

You will probably find, when you actually start putting a speech together, that you use several of these patterns in combination, with perhaps one serving to provide an overall outline. For example, in a speech about litter on school grounds, you might use a problem-solution pattern for your basic overall structure. But you might start out with an attention-getting remark ("Were you around the afternoon John Jones cut his head open on a broken bottle?") as in Monroe's Motivated Sequence. Then, in describing the problem, you might use a spatial pattern ("Let's walk around the school grounds and examine this situation"). Or you might choose a topical arrangement: (I) Litter from overflowing trash cans (II) Litter in parts of the grounds where there are no trash cans (III) Litter on special occasions, such as sports events with other schools, etc.). And you might use an inductive or deductive pattern to lead into your specific proposed solution.

Monroe's Motivated Sequence or the problem-solution pattern will probably be the most useful basic one to use, especially for persuasive speeches. For informative speeches and speeches to entertain, however, you may find a spatial or topical pattern provides the best overall structure. The important thing to remember is to experiment with these different methods of organization in order to find the ones which work best for your speech.

Purposeful Introductions

Now that you have an idea of how to put the main part of your speech together, let's backtrack a bit and examine ways in which you might begin it. First impressions are important keys to acceptability. People actually begin making judgments about you even before you begin to speak. Even stronger impressions are made by your introductory remarks. Since these initial remarks are so important, you should plan them carefully rather than assume that you will be blessed with a sudden bit of wit when you step up to the speaker's stand.

Introductions serve three basic purposes: (1) to gain attention, (2) to build the image of the speaker, and (3) to prepare the audience for the topic. A carefully designed introduction may accomplish all three purposes.

Some of the most effective introductory strategies are:

the startling statement
rhetorical questions
a humorous anecdote or a joke
reference to a current or historical event
a quotation
personal identification with the audience

A professor in a college freshman engineering course used to make effective use of the **startling statement** in his first lecture of the year. To stress the need for dedication and hard work, he told his students to "to look to the right of you and look to the left of you. One of the three of you will not finish this school year." Needless to say, his students were then prepared to listen to whatever suggestions he had to offer.

Rhetorical questions may be used to build suspense and make the audience feel personally involved in the speech. You ask the question, pause briefly to allow the audience to think about the question, and then supply your own answer. Unless you are very experienced and confident of your ability to think "on your feet," however, you should not encourage audience members to actually respond. One young lady in Missouri assumed that most people overlook their home state when planning a vacation. She asked for a show of hands of those who had vacationed in a Missouri city or state park within the past two years. Her next remark was to have been "Well, I see most of you are overlooking the diamonds in your own back yard." However, much to her surprise, all of her fellow students raised their hands. Bewildered, she bit her lower lip, picked up her illustrated poster of state parks, and struggled on with her speech.

Humorous anecdotes and **references to current events** are excellent techniques that may even be combined effectively. In 1973, a Democrat began his speech with a not-so-subtle reference to the Watergate scandal. "I must confess I'm nervous talking to you tonight with a visible microphone in front of me. Most of the microphones I've been speaking into lately have been hidden among flowers, behind pictures, or in my telephone."

A reference to a historical event served as an effective beginning for one of the most memorable speeches in our history. At an event now historic itself because of his remarks, Abraham Lincoln reminded his audience that "Fourscore and seven years ago, our fathers brought forth upon this continent a new nation, conceived in liberty. . . ."

Personal identification with an audience involves talking with an audience about things you've done together. You might also talk about problems that you and the audience have in common. If you were speaking at a pep rally, you might recall events from last year's rally and emphasize the contribution they made to the team's spirited victory. If you were speaking to a meeting of the PTA, you could stress that student problems are also problems for parents and teachers.

Using these strategies should focus attention on your speech, build your image, and give the audience a preview of your topic. Having accomplished this much, you will then be ready to move into the body of your speech.

☐ Write an introduction for each of the following topics.
   Don't use any one introductory strategy more than once.
      Parking Problems at School
      School Lunches
      Voting in Your First Election
      Reviving the Space Program
      Traveling in a Foreign Country
      _____ (Your Choice)

WRAP IT UP RIGHT

The most important thing about a conclusion is that it give a sense of completeness. The audience needs to sense that you have confidently reached the planned conclusion of your speech—not that you've just run out of things to say. Concluding remarks should be direct, specific, and spoken with assurance. In informative speeches, concluding remarks are frequently summaries of the main points of the speech or memorable quotes which contain the essence of the message. In a persuasive speech, you may conclude by visualizing the future, stressing how important the cause is to you and your audience, or emotionally urging the audience to take a specific course of action.

The conclusion—like the introduction—is so vital that it should be written out in advance. As your opening remarks make early impressions that influence your listeners, so your concluding remarks leave them with their final impression of you and your ideas. What kind of impression are you left with when the speaker shuffles around and finally says "Well, I guess that's about all I can say"? Certainly you're not impressed the way civil rights leader Dr. Martin Luther King's audience was when he concluded by quoting an old spiritual, "Free at last, free at last; Thank God Almighty we're free at last!"

Expressing Your Thoughts

Though your introduction and conclusion ought to be written out in advance, it is probably best to plan on delivering the rest of your speech from an outline. Memorizing is discouraged; it makes needless demands on your time and gives you the added pressure of having to remember lines. Reading your speech isn't a very good idea either. You'll remember your speech, but you may easily forget your audience. Wouldn't you rather be talked with than read to? What do you think of a speaker who reads to you about his personal experiences? Would an after-dinner speaker be funnier reading lines from a card—or sharing stories directly with the audience?

The extemporaneous method—speaking from a brief outline rather than from a manuscript—has the advantage of seeming more natural to those listening to you. Speaking extemporaneously, however, does not mean speaking without preparation or without carefully choosing the words you will use. In fact, because you will be using such brief notes, you need to think carefully in advance about the way you want to express your thoughts.

As you take notes for and practice your speech, you must be aware of the words you use and the effects those words can have on your listeners. This doesn't necessarily mean worrying about remembering *particular* words—though if you come up with a clever phrase in practice you might jot it down and use it. Instead, this means developing an awareness of oral language and a realization of how certain words may affect your audience.

Words Mean Different Things to Different People

It is important to remember that sometimes a word—even a very simple word—will draw different responses from your audience. For an example, consider the word *father*. For someone whose father was loving and kind, the mere word can bring a positive response. For someone whose father was unloving and unkind, the word *father* would immediately draw a negative response. To those who have known no father, the comparison may not provoke any sharp image or response. The meaning then lies not in the word *father*, but in the various experiences we have had with fathers.

USING WORDS ORALLY

Talking with an audience requires a kind of language different from that you would use in writing a report. In giving a public speech, you're talking with particular listeners who must quickly understand and remember what you say. This means that your language must be (1) appropriate for your particular listeners, (2) clear, and (3) memorable.

Appropriate Language

Common experiences may allow you to talk casually about flies, drops, and gels. While students with a theatrical background would understand such terms, students with no theater experience would have difficulty with such technical terms. If you must use words that are unfamiliar to your audience, make sure you define them. Jargon not understood is meaning not communicated.

Appropriate language also involves a careful use of slang. For a young person to use slang with an older audience is to risk obscuring meaning. For an older person to use slang with a young audience is to risk ridicule. Slang is basically a special language to identify members of an "in-group" and isolate those in the "out-group." It's hard—and not very effective—to use another group's language until you really feel a part of that group.

Clear Language

Your oral style must also be quickly comprehensible and clear to be effective. Keep in mind that the audience has only your spoken words, tone of voice, and "body language" to go on. This means you must express thoughts as briefly and simply as possible in order to get your meaning across to your listeners. It also means you should restate and summarize your central points—and be careful to use words with *specific*, rather than general, meanings.

How many times have you heard a speaker gripe about something like "all those lazy bums who bilk money from the government and then squander it"? Are the "lazy bums" the disabled veterans who lost the capacity to support themselves? Are they college students who receive federally sponsored loans? Retired people getting back some money from Social Security? People who for any number of reasons are unable to work and support themselves?

Besides being unclear, the "lazy bum" statement is also an example of loaded language. Loaded words are those chosen deliberately to appeal to the emotions. An audience will not think kindly about lazy bums, no matter who the speaker had in mind. Nor will the audience think kindly about people who "bilk" and "squander."

As a speaker you must be careful to avoid loaded words. They could backfire on you. Even if your meaning is clear, your audience will probably resent your using them. It could imply that you think the audience is ruled by its emotions, not its reasoning.

Making Meanings Memorable

Words and phrases are often memorable when they are used in ways that are different from the way we normally talk. Former Vice-President Spiro Agnew drew attention to his messages by using **alliteration.** For example, he once assailed his critics as "*n*attering *n*abobs of *n*egativism" and "*h*opeless *h*ysterical *h*ypochondriacs of *h*istory." Be careful, however, not to overdo it.

Memorable meanings may be achieved by **changing word order.** Most of us tend to fall into certain word-order patterns—subject, verb, object. That's fine in conversation, but in a speech varied word order can be an effective "attention holder" if it isn't overused. President John F. Kennedy's "Ask not what your country can do for you—ask what you can do for your country" is an example of unusual ordering of words. We usually say "don't ask" rather than "ask not." Kennedy's departure from our normal pattern helped make his wording memorable.

Metaphors may be used to dramatize a particular thought or feeling. Metaphor has traditionally been defined as an implied comparison. Modernists define it as any word or phrase used to create in your mind a picture that is different from the one normally created by the word or phrase. For example, you might say "the teacher was boiling mad." Just as a pot of boiling water is in a frenzied state of agitation, so any person when agitated beyond normal limits gets "boiling mad."

Have you ever heard someone say "We need to take the bull by the horns"? This metaphor makes the need to take decisive action more urgent and memorable than if the person had merely said, "We need to get to work on this."

One of the best stylistic devices may simply be the use of colorful words rather than bland ones. The meaning of a statement may be clearer when the speaker is described as *whispering, muttering, mumbling,* or *shouting* a slogan instead of just saying it.

A young baseball player once smashed a game-winning, inside-the-park home run. The next day the local paper carried a picture of him crossing home plate. Recognizing the need for vivid language, the newspaper did not say he "ran" across home plate. Instead, that memorable clipping says "Ewing huffed across home plate." Be vivid, but be kind!

SUMMING UP

The kinds of ideas you're talking about and the kinds of people you're talking with will influence the way you organize your thoughts and the words you use to express them. You should prepare an introduction that gains attention, builds your image, and prepares the audience for your topic. Any one of six introductory strategies can be used for these purposes: the startling statement, rhetorical questions, humorous ancedotes or jokes, references to current or historical events, quotations, or personal identification with the audience. The body of your speech may be organized according to one of several patterns: chronological, spatial, topical, problem-solution, deductive, inductive, or psychological.

Finally, your conclusion should let your audience know what points they should remember and that you have definitely finished saying what you intended to say.

Even though you speak extemporaneously—from a brief outline—you must express your organized thoughts in the best oral language you can. This means being aware that you and your audience may have different understandings of certain words. It also means trying to use words and phrases that are appropriate to your audience, clear, and memorable.

Activities

☐ Invite a local clergyman, lawyer, and political official to class. (If they can't come to class, maybe some of you could interview them at their offices and report results to the class.) Have them discuss the way they organize their ideas for speeches they give. Do they use one pattern consistently—or several? Do they speak extemporaneously? Why, or why not? Do they try to use particular words or phrases for particular purposes?

☐ What kinds of materials, of those mentioned in Chapter 2, do your guests usually use to try to support their ideas?

☐ Are there noticeable differences in speech preparation among the professionals? If so, why might this be?

☐ Find a speech that you might like (the magazine *Vital Speeches* is a good source), and report on it.
   What kind of introductory strategy did the speaker use?
   How was the speech concluded?
   Write down one example of
     alliteration
     unusual word order
     metaphor
     use of colorful words

☐ Your parents were probably top drawer cats who enjoyed tooling on downtown, avoided crude classmates and beatniks, and left neat friends with the promise to "see ya later, alligator." Their slang is history, and they probably don't understand much of your slang. Make a list of current slang words or phrases. Are there some audiences with whom, on some occasions, you could use these words? List them, along with appropriate occasions. When should such slang be avoided?

☐ Rewrite the following, putting it in more appropriate oral language. Compare your new version with others in the class.

    The Senator spoke a long time. As a consequence of his political elaborations the bill which was the subject of his verbose rhetoric was relegated from whence it had come.

☐ Organize your ideas for a five-minute speech. Turn in a paper explaining why you've organized your ideas the way you have. Start trying to put your ideas into words—that involves practicing delivering your speech—and that's the subject of the next chapter.

Bringing It All Together

4

How to deliver your speech

As important as the organization of your ideas and choice of words may be, the final impact of your speech will depend a great deal on the way you deliver it. An actress may have a fine script to work with and know her lines thoroughly—but if she delivers them poorly, the audience will be bored. A political candidate may have fine ideas but present them in such a lifeless way that people may look to his opponent for leadership. You may have had teachers who knew their subject well, but put half the class to sleep.

ESTABLISHING A POSITIVE IMAGE

Whether you are talking with another person or with a group, the way you present yourself and your message will have a lot to do with the response you receive.

It's important then for you to know how to present yourself in the best way possible—and the keys to such a presentation are *practice* and *preparation*. Be sure to practice your speech out loud—whether you practice by yourself, with a tape recorder, or in front of a parent or friend.

Practicing out loud gets you used to your own voice expressing the thoughts you'll share with an audience. You also get a better idea of how close you are to your time limit. It's best, of course, to practice in front of someone so that looking at people while sharing ideas will become a habit. Then too, your friend may be able to give you some helpful advice.

Excellent delivery of a speech involves:
- projecting the right appearance and attitude
- adjusting to the physical setting
- using your voice effectively
- using effective body language
- maintaining good eye contact with your audience.

APPEARANCE

One factor that influences the way people respond to others is appearance. Just as people expect certain speakers to talk about particular subjects, so they expect speakers to be dressed appropriately. A "good" dress or a suit and tie hardly seem necessary for the average classroom speech, but they're usually a must for a nominating speech at a major political convention. Appropriateness of dress and grooming is based on what others expect and what they will accept. If you appear so sloppily or so formally dressed that you and your audience feel uncomfortable with one another, then your chances of communicating effectively are slim.

CONTROLLING STAGE FRIGHT

Feeling that others will accept the *outward you*—the way you're dressed—will probably give you more confidence that they will accept the message—your speech—given by the *inner you*. Yet, most people, if they really care about what they're doing, have feelings of anxiety about being able to do well. Many successful actors, athletes, and speakers have said that they felt some nervousness before appearing in public.

Most speakers have doubts about how well they'll do when speaking. The fact that you're worried about giving your speech isn't unusual—your teacher is probably worried about the presentations he or she makes to your class. Some speakers and actors say that stage fright actually makes them feel more alert. You probably won't be able to get rid of it entirely, but you can learn to understand it and control it.

Our greatest fear is probably the fear of the unknown. What will it be like? What will I say? You can reduce this fear by being well prepared and by practicing. You should realize though that no one is perfect—everybody makes mistakes. The most experienced speakers have shown their slides in the wrong order or upside down, gotten their "tangs tongueled," dropped their notes on the floor, and coughed through half their speech. What can you do when something like this happens? Smile, correct the situation, and go on. Or—if the problem is not as obvious as dropped note cards—figure that few people, if any, noticed the mistake and proceed with your speech.

A ten-year-old boy who stuttered went to a university for help. The clinician who was to help the boy told him he'd work with him only if he wanted to become the world's best stutterer. Puzzled, the boy agreed to follow the clinician's advice. The youngster was told to attend the classes of the ten best professors at the university and mark down the number of times they stuttered—repeated words and sounds and were otherwise "non-fluent" in their speech. To the youngster's surprise, he had several instances to mark down for each professor. He was also surprised to notice that the professors weren't bothered by the non-fluencies—and neither were the students. Communication was effective.

What's the point of this true story? If your hands are sweating, or your knees knocking, or if you stumble over some words, you're not alone. The point is—you can go on and communicate effectively. Many problems which seem great to the speaker aren't even noticed by the audience.

If you're still a little uptight, try taking a few deep breaths or clenching and unclenching your fists before getting up to speak. While speaking, put your nervous energy to work by walking around a little or by gesturing. If you don't overdo it, such activities will make your speech seem more natural—and they'll also help you relax!

Projecting a Confident Attitude

Your audience is more likely to believe in you if you seem to believe in your ideas yourself. It's important therefore to approach your audience with apparent confidence. As you approach the speaking area take firm, definite steps rather than shuffling your feet. Hold your head up and look at people in the audience rather than at the ink stains on the floor. A nice smile before you begin speaking tends to reassure the audience that you're pleased to have the opportunity to share some ideas with them. Remember attitudes and behavior are like germs in a crowded room—they spread quickly. If you look bored with the whole affair, your audience is more likely to become bored with you. But if you seem excited about talking with them, they'll be more likely to be excited about listening to you.

Adjusting to the Communication Setting

Many times you won't know beforehand the size of the room, whether or not you'll have a microphone, or even whether or not you'll have a lectern (speaker's stand) to put your notes on. The key to being able to adapt to whatever you find lies in preparing your speech with flexibility. For instance, placing your speech notes on 3 x 5 cards gives you flexibility; you can easily hold them in your hand if no lectern is available. And, if you're using a microphone, note cards won't make rustling and crackling sounds to be heard in the fartherest corner of the room. Since you can hold note cards, they also give you the freedom to move closer to your audience if the room is set up so you can (and if you want to).

If you are using a microphone, it is important that you continue to speak with the audience, and that you do not focus on the mike. The mike is simply to help you be heard easier; let it help you do the work. Speak in a normal tone and avoid great changes in volume. Don't stand too close to the mike—the best distance depends on the mike used. If you have a chance, try out the mike before the audience arrives.

Because microphones magnify normal sounds, avoid doing things that will produce distracting noises. Don't touch or tap the mike. Don't cough or clear your throat while facing the microphone. Finally, avoid wearing any loose jewelry, especially metal, that will produce loud clattering and clanking that will echo throughout the room.

Of Platforms and Podiums

Speaking from an elevated stage establishes a certain physical and psychological distance between speaker and audience. This distance tends to add to the speaker's "air of authority" but it also hurts any attempts to be conversational with an audience. This same problem exists when a lectern is available. If you believe an informal approach is important, you can create more of that feeling by moving in front of the lectern.

Your height and the lectern's will also determine where you stand. If you appear either to be peeping over the lectern or about to trip over it, your audience will certainly be amused, perhaps so much so that they can't concentrate on your speech. So judge the height of the lectern carefully as you approach it. If it is too tall or short for you, adjust it before you begin speaking. If it can't be adjusted, speak in front or to the side of the lectern.

If you do speak from behind a lectern, it's important that you use it rather than letting it use you. Don't let it inhibit your movements and gestures. Movement keeps an audience alert, whereas a slumping, tired posture encourages a similar attitude on the part of your listeners. You may rest your hands, but not all your weight, on the speaker's stand. This presents an alert, balanced picture and frees your hands to gesture at a level that can be seen by audience members.

Adjusting to Seating Patterns

Most speakers have a natural tendency to seek out friendly, responsive faces in their audiences. This seems a good idea, particularly for the beginning speaker, because it is encouraging to look at a friendly face. However, you should try to talk with all sections of your audience and not concentrate on one side of the room or one group of people throughout your whole speech. If you do that, the people you don't look at will feel left out.

If you switch focus from person to person (or side to side) too rapidly, however, you'll look like a fan at a ping-pong match! Instead, concentrate on one person, or area, long enough to explain one idea or example. Then switch to another person, or area, for your next idea or example—and so on, idea by idea.

There may be times when it would be a good idea to ask people to move to another section of the room. If your whole audience is clustered in the back two rows or split into two camps, one on each side of the room, and no one in the middle, it's going to be difficult for you to talk with them. For effective communication, speaker and audience should be close enough so that no one has to strain to see or hear. Audience members should be close enough to each other to feel like a unit—a group sharing ideas instead of a series of isolated individuals who are too far apart to share. So if your audience is far away or scattered, ask them to come forward or to the center section. By doing that, you will probably increase their alertness and make it easier for them to focus their attention on you.

☐ List audiences that you could talk with effectively while wearing jeans. List audiences, or occasions, that require you to wear "better" clothes.

☐ What differences would there be in your responses if the following spoke to your class about their work (a) in uniform (b) out of uniform:
    a military person
    a police officer
    a nurse
    a telephone repairman

☐ What things could your class do as an audience that would help a speaker control stage fright?

☐ Do you feel differently about a teacher who always speaks from behind a desk or lectern and a teacher who moves around the room while sharing ideas? What difference would this make to you in the way you would listen and interact?

☐ Watch a live or televised speech. Report (orally) to the class on:
    the topic, and its suitability to the audience and the occasion
    the speaker's organization and use of words
    the speaker's dress, apparent confidence, and use of the communication setting

Using Your Voice Effectively

Earlier we noted that words mean different things to different people. In the same way, different *nonverbal* signals mean different things to different people. There's an old song that warned (or promised) "every little movement has a meaning all its own." That is true not only of every little movement or gesture but also of each variation in vocal characteristics: *quality, pitch, volume,* and *rate.* Variations in these vocal characteristics may be used to hold attention, to emphasize key ideas, and to create the desired emotional atmosphere.

Your voice sounds the way it does partly because of your physical make-up and partly because of the way you've developed it over the years. Your voice is also tied in with your personality, so you're not likely to change it dramatically overnight. However, if you want to make your voice more pleasant or forceful you can—if you're willing to put in the effort.

Quality Quality is that characteristic of your voice which makes it different from other voices. The basic quality of your voice is determined primarily by the size, shape, and texture of the lining of your mouth, nose, and throat. Obviously you can't change those things, though you can to some degree vary your vocal quality.

Your primary aim as a public speaker is to project a pleasant quality that doesn't detract from your message. This means avoiding common problems like excessive nasality (talking "through the nose"), or excessive breathiness (using more air than voice; at its most extreme, breathiness becomes whispering).

It is impossible here to give specific instructions for correcting individual problems; your teacher will probably be able to assist if you need special help. But in general, try to:

> open your mouth wide enough when you speak to allow free passage of air and sound
> breathe naturally—not in short gasps or deep shudders
> stand straight, with your feet firmly on the ground; remember that your whole body can help "support" your voice.

Pitch The pitch of your voice is determined by the speed with which your vocal folds (often called vocal "cords") vibrate. Like a guitar or any other stringed instrument, the faster the rate of vibration, the higher the pitch; the slower the rate, the lower the pitch. The rate of vibration of the vocal folds is determined by some physical things you can't control —thickness, length, and elasticity of the folds—and some you can—degree of tension in them and the amount of breath pressure applied.

Changes in the pitch of the voice give meaning to speech. When speakers are really interested in their subject, they unconsciously vary their pitch to give emphasis to certain words and subordinate others. These variations in pitch also help hold attention. A speech delivered on one note is about as exciting as a song sung on one note!

To develop greater flexibility of vocal quality and pitch, try some of the following exercises.

☐ Say "Yes, dear" in various ways in order to convey the following emotions: boredom, eagerness, irritation, love, sarcasm, and weariness.

☐ Begin counting on as low a pitch as you can and then go as high as you can without straining your voice. Reverse the process—start counting on as high a pitch as you can and go as low as you can. How "high" can you count? Try this every day for a week and see if you can count any higher or lower.

☐ Varying your quality and pitch, say
"The time is coming when we must make some changes" as: an authoritarian employer, a person about to retire, a minister, a candidate for student council.
"Dinner is on the table" as: an angry parent, a tired waitress, a loving spouse, you to a brother or sister.
"What grade did you make on that test?" as: an interested friend, a surprised friend, a sarcastic classmate, a teacher who forgot to record your grade.

☐ Read each pair of words twice. First, read the first word high-pitched and the second low-pitched and then read the first word low-pitched and the second high-pitched.

Go home
Right now
That's right
You know

☐ Examine a guitar—or other stringed instrument—in class. What are the differences in the strings that produce low pitches and those that produce higher ones? How can the pitch of one string be raised or lowered?

Volume It is obvious that if your message can't be heard, it can't be understood. If you breathe well enough to climb stairs, dance, and play intramural sports, you breathe well enough to make yourself heard.

Changes in volume can be used to give emphasis to ideas. Speakers usually give special emphasis to those words which (1) introduce new ideas, (2) stress repeated thoughts, (3) build to a climax, and (4) compare or contrast. By increasing or lowering your volume, you may focus attention upon a vitally important concept.

Rate A fast rate of speech usually conveys a feeling of excitement and vitality. A slow rate may indicate calm confidence. Your rate tends to reflect your mood and personality. In a public speech your rate needs to be varied—within reason; try to avoid extremes. Basically, your best rate of speech is the one you feel most comfortable with—as long as your listeners still understand you easily.

One useful rhetorical device that is often overlooked is ...... the pause. Many people are so afraid of silence that they feel compelled to fill any void with some sound, no matter how lacking in meaning: "Like, ...uh, ...mmmmm, uh, ..ya know!" A pause *between ideas* may clarify meaning or provide emphasis. A pause *before a word* tends to heighten suspense as it draws attention to the "coming attraction." A pause *after a thought* encourages the listener to reflect on his interpretation of the message.

- ☐ To improve breathing, inhale slowly for five seconds and then exhale at the same rate. Repeat until you can do it easily and steadily.

- ☐ Inhale as above, but begin counting out loud as you exhale. How far can you count on one breath? See if you can count five or ten numbers more by practicing for a week.

- ☐ Say "Get out of the way, please" to:
    someone next to you
    someone five feet away
    someone fifty feet away
    someone two hundred feet away
  Did your other vocal characteristics change as you increased volume? Did you quit saying "please" at some point? If so, why?

PLEASE !

BODY LANGUAGE

During your next lunch break, take time to observe the people and conversations around you. Which people seem to be the focus of attention at the various tables? How are they sitting? What are they doing with their hands? What kinds of expressions are registered on their faces?

Just as there are certain words and styles of dress that are expected in certain situations, so there are postures, movements, and gestures that are the accepted norm in particular schools. However, speaking in front of a large group of people usually calls for you to be more alert and active than in informal conversation.

Variations in movement, hand gestures, and facial expression tend to gain our attention. In addition to gaining attention, body language gives emphasis to ideas. A request to leave the room becomes an order when the person speaking tightens his or her facial muscles, and points a finger toward the door.

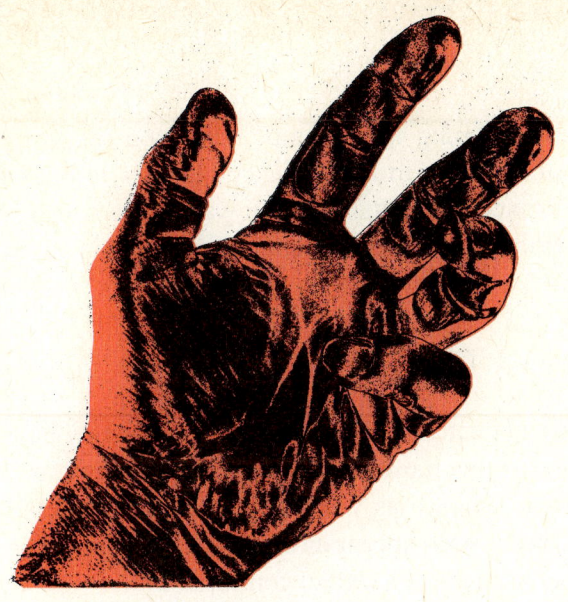

Gestures may do more than give emphasis to ideas—they may convey ideas. A policeman directing traffic uses certain gestures and you know he means "Stop, then turn right." A basketball referee uses certain gestures and you know a Buck was running with the ball and it will be the Celtics' ball going the other way. You may use gestures to signal "It's OK," "Peace," or "Cool it." When speaking publicly you can use gestures to convey ideas as long as you're sure your audience will understand their meaning.

A speaker can use gestures to help describe people, objects, and activities. Imagine trying to describe a struggle to catch a fish or an exciting touchdown run without any gestures or body movement! You can use the same types of body language when speaking in front of a group as you do when talking with a friend in the hall. However, since you're further from your audience in a public speaking situation, you need to make your movements and gestures fuller and more distinct. Make sure your gestures can be seen above the speaker's stand and by the people in the back row.

The Eyes Have It

People may make many judgments about you and your feelings on the basis of what they see in your facial expressions and eyes. Most of us believe that others are interested in us if they look at us while we're talking, and that they're not interested in us if they look around the room or at the floor. Keeping this in mind, the good speaker establishes *eye contact* with individuals in his audience in order to hold their attention better. Eye contact is also the primary way that you can judge audience responses in order to make any needed adjustments in content or delivery.

SUMMING UP

Communicating effectively calls for more than merely having good ideas —it calls for delivering those ideas well. Such delivery comes with practice and increased confidence as you learn to control stage fright. Effective delivery is easier if your appearance and the physical setting of the room allow you and the audience to feel comfortable with one another. As the speaker, you should encourage whatever adjustments are called for to make the setting conducive to effective communication.

Effective delivery holds attention, clarifies ideas, and helps give proper emphasis to key ideas. These functions of effective delivery are best attained by

> maintaining good eye contact with your audience
> an alert but relaxed posture and varied movements and gestures
> a voice loud enough to be heard and understood
> a voice pleasant enough to listen to and varied enough that people will pay attention

Activities

☐ Pick a topic for a five-minute persuasive speech in which you will try to
- sell your audience a product

or

- convince your audience that something should be changed (a traffic law, for example, or a school or town policy)

or

- get your audience to perform some action (give money to a certain charity, attend a sports or entertainment event, etc.)

☐ Research your topic carefully.

☐ Organize your thoughts and prepare a careful introduction and conclusion, choosing words which will express your thoughts and convince your audience.

☐ Rehearse your speech, paying attention to how you use your voice, body language, and what you know of the communication setting.

☐ Deliver your speech. Remember to dress appropriately and to use eye contact.

☐ After everyone in class has given his or her speech, vote on which three speeches were the most convincing: Which ones really made you want to buy the product, support the proposed change, or go out and do what the speaker asked?

☐ Discuss, in terms of the principles covered in the last four chapters, what factors in each of the three "best" speeches were handled the most successfully. Which were handled less successfully?

AUDIENCE FEEDBACK 5

How to use it and give it

Responses from audience members are referred to as *feedback*. Feedback may be verbal—

BOO! **Right On!** **Amen!**

or it may be nonverbal— ☹ Feedback is frequently given after a speech: "That was a fine sermon, Reverend Neth." "That was a dumb idea, Bob!" But feedback is also an ongoing process during a speech. Alertness to the kinds of feedback you are receiving may help you make adjustments that will improve communication between you and your audience.

"Neutral" Feedback

The most devastating feedback is the kind that indicates you and your message are being ignored. Better to have everyone disagree with your choices for this year's Oscars than to be totally ignored by the group. Pity the speaker who looks at people who are whispering to one another, reading notes, or staring out the windows. Such "neutral" feedback cries out for adjustments on the part of the speaker. If you're speaking, you can move about more to gain attention—even, in some situations, move about in the audience. You can make greater use of variety in style and delivery—use some humor, more slang or more challenging language; use the chalkboard, vary your volume—anything that seems to work. Finally, you may attempt to gain back the audience by pointing out how important your topic is to their interests and well-being.

Negative Feedback

Feedback may be obviously negative—a frown, a person shaking his or her head no, or verbal heckling. Such negative feedback at least indicates that the audience thinks you and your ideas are worthy of a certain kind of attention! If you anticipate negative reactions, as you may if you know your point of view is unpopular with certain people, you may organize your remarks so that you first explain the opposition's point of view and then contrast it with yours. That will at least let the audience know that you understand, and have thought about, their viewpoint. During the speech, avoid inflammatory language and an overly dramatic delivery—either can offend. Most important, if your audience grows hotter, *you* stay cool!

Positive Feedback

Naturally, you hope your feedback will be positive—smiles, vocal encouragement, or applause. In such cases you may just give your audience more of the same—but not too much more. Samuel Clemens told of listening five minutes to such a fired-up preacher that he was prepared to drop $5 in the collection plate. After ten minutes he thought $10 would be more appropriate. Twenty minutes later he decided $5 was right after all. Thirty minutes later he was thinking $1 would be enough. An hour later, when the collection plate was finally passed around, Clemens took out $5!

One form of positive feedback that can be difficult to handle is laughter. The first thing to do when the laughter starts is—pause. When the laughter begins to die down then you can begin speaking again at a slower rate, gradually resuming your normal rate as the audience quiets down. In starting up after the pause, it's also a good idea to speak louder and in a higher pitch to signal the audience that you're ready to go on.

MEANWHILE, IN THE AUDIENCE

Although you'll be making several speeches in this class and will no doubt find opportunities to speak in public in the future, you will still probably spend more time in the audience listening than on the platform speaking. Listening well doesn't just involve showing up and sitting quietly while someone else talks. Just as it takes knowledge and practice to improve your speaking skills, so you should be aware of certain principles and *practice them* if you want to improve as a listener.

A good listener listens for the *main ideas* of a speech. Don't waste your time trying to write down, or remember, every detail—it may keep you from hearing the speaker's key idea.

To be a good listener you must be a selfish listener. Listen carefully to the entire speech. Even if you start off thinking there's nothing in the speech for you, you might miss something if you let your mind wander. Try to avoid distractions—the note-passing two rows in front of you, and the kids playing ball outside. Focus your attention on the speaker's ideas.

Avoid over-reacting. You may be upset by the speaker's proposal to lengthen the school day, but closing your mind to the idea won't help you gain a thing. Besides you might miss a point that would cause you to agree; maybe the speaker favors lengthening the school day in order to bring about a four-day school week. A good principle to follow is to hear the speaker out before you judge the message or the person.

If the speaker is trying to persuade you to do something, it's important that you test the materials used to support his or her ideas. You may use the same tests that were mentioned in Chapter 2:

Do the examples used by the speaker really support the ideas?
Are quoted sources worthy of belief?
Are the comparisons and analogies used really fair and accurate?
Are statistics and other materials up to date?
Are they representative of the situation as you know it?

As a listener you will be aware not only of what the speaker says, but also of how he or she says it. You will be aware of the speaker's voice, nervousness or poise, body language, and general rapport with the audience. These factors will have an influence on how you react to the speaker.

Responsible listeners also need to give appropriate feedback to speakers, because a speaker can be affected by the speech as much as audience members. The speaker's ideas can be reinforced by positive feedback and changed by negative feedback. Especially in a persuasive speech, you as a listener can play an active part in bringing about change or accepting or rejecting an idea—if you provide the speaker with feedback.

A Feedback Experiment

☐ Prepare a one- to two-minute speech on your favorite movie or TV show. You can be as entertaining as the show, inform us as to what it is about, or try to persuade us to see it when we can—the purpose of your speech will be up to you.

The purpose of the exercise will be to practice adapting to audience feedback. Your teacher may plant some "neutrals," negatives, and positives—your task will be to win over as many of them as possible.

☐ When you are part of a feedback group, react, as assigned, to each "speech." Keep your feedback natural—no booing, no cheering.

☐ After all the speeches have been made, the speakers should describe what the effects of various kinds of feedback were on them. Did you change what you had planned to say as a result of feedback? What changes did you make, if any? Did you deliver your speech to a particular listener? Which one and why?

MONDAY MORNING REFLECTIONS

Life goes on after a championship game—whether you win or lose. So it goes on after a speech. The important thing is to take time to evaluate what the game, or speech, has meant to all the participants. College and professional football teams gather on Mondays to study videotape replays of their most recent game. Their goal is not to dwell on the mistakes and glories of that game, but to see what they can learn from them in order to do better next time.

If your school has a videotape recorder, you can watch yourself make speeches and evaluate what you have done. But even if your school doesn't have one, each time you make a speech, you can learn something from it that will help you next time. Ask yourself: what kinds of supportive materials seemed most effective? Did audience members understand you and your ideas easily? If you will be speaking to the same group again, what do you now know about their responses that will help next time?

Popular singers practice intensively before every performance. Top big-league hitters take hours of batting practice during spring training and continue to refine their swings during the season. Similarly, the person who is interested in entertaining others or in making his or her ideas heard must continue to work hard before every speaking opportunity. You can't skimp on advance preparation and audience analysis and expect to be effective. Effective public speaking results from applying what you learn from each experience to the preparation and delivery of the next speech.

SUMMING UP

Audience responses are referred to as *feedback*. Feedback may be verbal or nonverbal. You receive some feedback after a speech and much feedback during a speech. A speaker must learn to adapt to three kinds of audience feedback—"neutral," negative, and positive.

Since you'll probably be a listener more often than a public speaker, it's important to improve your ability to listen. This improvement can result from: listening for key ideas, being a "selfish" listener, ignoring distractions, avoiding overreactions to speaker or message, and applying critical tests to the evidence used by any speaker.

Life goes on. There will be more speeches to give and to listen to. The important thing is to learn from what you've done so the next speech will be even better.

Activities

☐ Prepare and deliver an eight- to ten-minute speech. After (*not* during) each speech, listeners should fill out an evaluation form similar to the one printed at the end of this section. Each speaker should evaluate his or her speech on a form too.

☐ Your teacher will collect the evaluation forms, and read them, remove the evaluators' names and give at least five representative one to each speaker.

☐ As a speaker, compare in writing your self-evaluation with those you received from the audience. Are there big differences of opinion? Do you agree on needed improvements? Do you agree on particular strengths? Did the audience feedback during your speech have any effect on what you did? If so, describe the changes.

SPEECH EVALUATION FORM

Speaker _____ Date _____

Circle the number you think is appropriate. In the space provided, write your own additional comments.

Purpose	1 not clear	2	3	4	5 clear
Topic	1 uninteresting	2	3	4	5 interesting
Introduction	1 dull	2	3	4	5 attention-getting
Supportive Materials	1 inappropriate	2	3	4	5 appropriate
Organization	1 illogical	2	3	4	5 logical
Words Used	1 inappropriate	2	3	4	5 appropriate
Delivery	1 dull	2	3	4	5 dynamic
General Effectiveness	1 not informative	2	3	4	5 informative

Evaluator's Name _____

SPEAKER EVALUATION FORM

Speaker _____ Date _____

Check the comments you think are appropriate. In the space provided, write your own comments.

General Appearance	Very Good	Good	Needs Improvement

Use of Voice		Very Good	Good	Needs Improvement
	quality			
	pitch			
	volume			
	rate			

Body Language		Very Good	Good	Needs Improvement
	movements			
	gestures			
	facial expressions			

Eye Contact			

Evaluator's Name _____

Section 2

The Challenge Of Pleasant Disagreement

6

How to write a debate proposition for classroom use

Have you ever wanted to see a musical comedy when your friends wanted to see a horror movie? Have you ever asked for an extra day before handing in an outline for a history paper and had your teacher refuse? Or, on the basis of your argument, has a teacher ever extended a deadline?

It's unlikely that a day will go by when you don't express an opinion that is different from one held by a friend or teacher. The United States Supreme Court is composed of nine of the ablest minds in our country and yet they often find themselves disagreeing by votes of 5-4 on important decisions. Reasonable people can disagree about almost anything.

One of the most reasonable ways to test opposite viewpoints is through debate. As former debate coach Jake Hoover used to stress, "debate is the art of pleasant disagreement." To paraphrase the Greek philospher Plato, enemies quarrel to destroy one another—while friends debate among themselves for their better instruction.

There is a difference, then, in "arguing down" a friend and "debating with" that friend. To "argue down" is to seek to put the other person down—to force that person to comply with your viewpoint. Such a tactic—whether done in front of a locker or in front of a speech class—is not to be confused with debate.

Debate—wherever it takes place—avoids personality clashes and places the emphasis upon testing a particular conclusion. When most people think of formal debate, they think primarily of an activity limited to high school and college students. It is certainly true that most traditional debates take place in educational settings. But debate techniques are used in the "real" world as well as in the classroom and at tournaments. Lawyers "debate" in court; legislators "debate" in the House and Senate; political candidates "debate" on TV. You yourself, in a sense, "debate" whenever you and a friend calmly exchange opposing views on a single issue. Training in debate—whether gained in classroom debates or tournament debating—focuses on developing the skills to logically test and support particular positions.

Phrasing the Debate Proposition

The subject of a debate—the issue—is put in a carefully worded statement called a *proposition*. Traditionally, in classroom and tournament debates, debate propositions are worded in the same way. Debate propositions, for example, start off like this:

Resolved: That

After the "That" comes a clear, concise statement of the conclusion that one side wants accepted.

Resolved: That federal highway funds should be made available to develop systems of public transportation.

(Just as there are two sides—at least—in an argument, there are two sides in a debate. One of these, called the *affirmative* side, argues *for* the proposition. The other side, the *negative*, argues *against* it. It is traditional to state the proposition in terms of the affirmative side.)

There are five basic rules for phrasing a debate topic.

1. The proposition should focus on *one central idea*. An unacceptable proposition would be "Resolved: That Indiana should have no-fault auto insurance and lower its speed limit to 50 mph." To attempt to debate two issues, whether they are related or not, creates needless confusion. You also can't very well outline alternatives. You can't be *resolved* to do one thing *or* another thing. It wouldn't make too much sense to say "Resolved: That we build a new school auditorium—or fix up the old one." It's much better to debate one issue at a time.

2. The proposition should be affirmative in *intent*. That is, the topic should be phrased so that the affirmative side will be supporting a change in the *status quo*—in the way things are now. For instance, the way things are now the President of the United States is elected to a four-year term of office, and may serve two such four-year terms. Someone wanting a change in the *status quo* might move the adoption of the proposition: "Resolved: That the President of the United States should hold office for one six-year term." By definition, the affirmative side will support this specific change while the negative side will oppose it.

3. The proposition should be *stated* affirmatively. Negative statements are confusing. How about this: "Resolved: That our state *not* legalize pari-mutuel betting." Because the affirmative side always argues *for* the proposition, if you're on that side you are going to have to argue *against* pari-mutuel betting. If you're on the negative side and therefore have to argue *against* the proposition, you're going to have to argue *for* pari-mutuel betting. Confusing? You bet—much the way a double negative is in grammar!

4. The proposition should be stated in *neutral language.* Heavily loaded emotional language gives one side an unreasonable advantage and the other a near impossible task. For instance, the proposition "Resolved: That no United States citizen should die from lack of sufficient medical care" places an almost impossible burden on the negative. Who can oppose medical care to save lives? By resolving instead "That the federal government should provide essential medical care to all citizens at public expense," neither side will be at a disadvantage because of the wording of the proposition. The negative can be against the proposition without appearing inhuman.

5. The proposition should be phrased *clearly* and precisely. To be "Resolved: That there ought to be some changes made around our school" is to be so vague as to resolve nothing. The proposition should state clearly and specifically what change is proposed.

☐ Break up into small groups. Discuss whether the following debate propositions are phrased properly. Be sure to give reasons for your decisions.

    a. Resolved: That alimony payments should not be done away with in divorce decisions.
    b. Resolved: That our community should spend more on public education and that downtown parking fees should be increased.
    c. Resolved: That the United States Constitution should be amended.
    d. Resolved: That math not be required for high school graduation.
    e. Resolved: That those inconsiderate, sloppy citizens who thoughtlessly litter our streets be sentenced to one day's service with the city sanitation department for each violation.

☐ Defend your decisions before the class as a whole. (You can do this as a group or you can pick a spokesperson to present your group's case.)

☐ Working in the same groups, write three possible debate propositions and read them to the class. Have the class discuss whether or not the propositions are properly phrased. Have one person keep all propositions the class approves for future use.

TYPES OF PROPOSITIONS

The issues you debate vary in importance and in type. For example, you debate with classmates about what the principal did and did not say at yesterday's assembly. You debate with friends over which recording artist is "absolutely" the best. You may debate with your parents about family curfew policy. These three "debates" revolve around "propositions" of (1) fact, (2) value, and (3) policy.

Propositions of Fact A proposition of fact is simply a statement, in proposition form, that something is true:

Resolved: That state employment practices are discriminatory.

Resolved: That Joe Doe killed Phil Doe.

Debating a proposition of fact requires you to demonstrate objectively that something exists, is true, or did happen. Decisions in a court of law, for example, are based on what arguments a judge or jury believes to be closest to the truth.

Propositions of Value Trying to decide which movie is the best of the year is not a decision based on fact; it is based on value judgments—beliefs and opinions. "Resolved: That Robert Redford should win an Academy Award" would be a proposition of value. If you were on the affirmative side of a debate on that proposition, you should first explain your criteria—judging standards—for an Academy-Award-winning performance. Then, you should show how Robert Redford lives up to your criteria.

Propositions of Policy Policy propositions are those which call for some particular action to be taken in the future. An example of a policy proposition would be: "Resolved: That two fine arts credits should be required for high school graduation." As you may note, policy propositions also involve issues of fact and value. In this case, the definition of fine arts, would be largely a matter of fact, and the worth of such courses would depend on your values. The factor that makes this proposition one of policy is that is calls for some form of *action*.

☐ Classify the following as propositions of fact, value, or policy.

1. Resolved: That many movies rated GP are worse than most rated R.
2. Resolved: That Congress should take action to outlaw the manufacture and sale of handguns.
3. Resolved: That smoking is a sin.
4. Resolved: That smoking is harmful to your health.
5. Resolved: That smoking in public places should be illegal.

6. Resolved: That contributions of minorities have been ignored in most history texts.
7. Resolved: That woman's place is in the home.
8. Resolved: That our form of government is superior to any other.
9. Resolved: That the United States Government should discontinue foreign aid.
10. Resolved: That nuclear power generation is as safe as conventional fossil fuel.

Most debates in educational settings are on policy propositions. Policy propositions are used because they concern taking actions that can lead to important consequences. Examples of policy propositions recently debated by high school debate teams are:

Resolved: That the United States should establish a system of compulsory service by all citizens.

Resolved: That the federal government should establish, finance, and administer programs to control air and water pollution in the United States.

Resolved: That the jury system in the United States should be significantly changed.

Resolved: That all federal elective officials' campaign funds should be provided exclusively by the federal government.

In high school tournament debating, each year's topic is chosen months in advance by high school coaches across the country.* Inside the classroom though, you may be asked to debate a topic you pick yourself. So what do you choose? Probably a policy question—about something *current, controversial,* and *complex.*

---

* For information, write to the National University Extension Association, Committee on Discussion and Debate, 68 Prince Lucien Campbell, University of Oregon, Eugene, Oregon 97403.

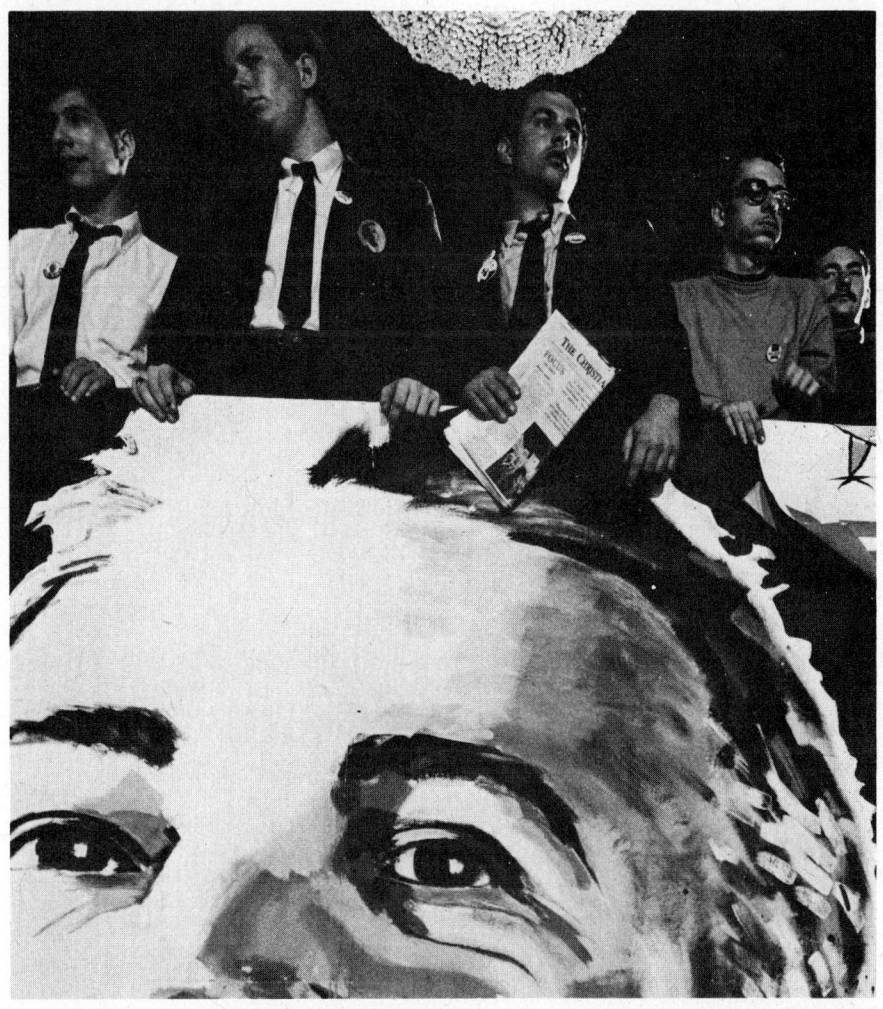

Policy debates are most exciting when they deal with a *current* problem. There may be a wealth of material on an outdated topic like admitting China to the United Nations or allowing eighteen-year-olds to vote, but the information won't be very enlightening for debaters or their audience. They'll probably already know how both those issues were decided. But if you pick an issue no one's solved yet, there's a chance that your debate could lead to someone's taking action for or against the proposition—action which might one day influence a real solution of a current problem.

Topics should also be *controversial*. If everyone agrees, there is no need for debate. Controversy results from serious problems that create at least two vigorous points of view. "Resolved: That the schools should educate young people" just has no place to go. It's not worth your research time or the audience's listening time if you don't deal with a topic controversial enough to be exciting.

A debate proposition should be based on a *complex* issue. It's ridiculous to debate an issue that hinges on easily obtainable facts. You don't have to debate about what movie is showing at your neighborhood theater—you can call and find out! You don't have to debate which state is the most populous; you can look it up in the *World Almanac*. What about "Resolved: That the federal government should eliminate farm subsidies"? That's not nearly so simple. To debate on either side of that one would take enough thought to make it a worthwhile project for everyone concerned.

☐ Answer the following individually—you may need to do research for some—and then compare your answers with others in class.
What school problems would make good debate topics?
What problems exist in your community that you would like to debate?
What problems are currently being debated in your state legislature? In the United States Congress?

☐ Evaluate each suggested topic in terms of its being current, controversial, and complex.

☐ Pick three topics and phrase them as propositions of policy. Which do you think would make the most interesting debate? Why?

Despite what we've just said, not all classroom debates have to be limited to burning public issues. As a matter of fact, they don't even have to be limited to current issues—not if they are either *literary* or *historical*.

LITERARY DEBATE

Literary debates can deal with propositions of fact, value, or policy. A literary proposition of *fact*, for example, might seek to establish the real authorship of particular works. Did Shakespeare really write all the plays attributed to him? A literary proposition of *value* might allow class members to debate the merits of reading Ray Bradbury over the merits of reading Kurt Vonnegut, Jr. To take literary debate a step further, you might debate whether TV drama and comedy shows are portraying blacks fairly. A literary proposition of *policy* might focus on what kinds of literature should be emphasized in English classes. Or what kinds of plays the drama club should present.

☐ Think of a movie or TV show that you've seen lately that was controversial. What was controversial about it? What might be gained by debating the theme of the show?

or

☐ What story or book have you read that might be used in a literary debate?

☐ Using either of the above, write a proposition for a literary debate. State your proposition to the class. Tell them whether it is one of fact, value, or policy. If they don't agree, find out why and try to reach agreement.

HISTORICAL DEBATE

Historical debate can also be used in the classroom. In this case, you pick a topic of historical importance. *Value* propositions might center on the pros and cons of such decisions as that of President Truman to drop atomic bombs on Hiroshima and Nagasaki, or the decision of the Soviet Union to exile the controversial author Aleksandr Solzhenitsyn.

You can give *policy* propositions a special twist by role-playing, if you want. How about debating the ideal form of the United States government as viewed by Alexander Hamilton—with Thomas Jefferson on the opposing side.

☐ Break up into small groups. Suggest some historical events that might be interesting topics for historical debates—perhaps some specific decision to enter a war, to declare independence, to amend a Constitution, or to hold back or grant human rights.

☐ Think of a historical debate that your class might role-play or recreate.
  Webster–Calhoun
  Lincoln–Douglas
  Kennedy–Nixon
  _____ (your choice)

☐ Perhaps, combining literary debate and historical debate, you might do a scene of courtroom debate from *Inherit the Wind,* by Jerome Lawrence and Robert E. Lee. The courtroom scene in which Clarence Darrow cross-examines William Jennings Bryan is an interesting study in debate technique.

SUMMING UP

Debate is a reasonable way of testing particular conclusions. The affirmative side proposes the particular change in the *status quo,* and the negative side opposes it. The change being proposed is called a debate proposition.

There are five rules to follow in phrasing a proposition so that the issues of the debate will be clear to everyone. A debate proposition should:

1. have one central idea,
2. be affirmative in intent,
3. be stated affirmatively,
4. be stated in neutral language, and
5. be phrased clearly and precisely.

There are three types of propositions—*fact, value,* and *policy.* Most classroom debates use propositions of policy because they focus on possible future actions that may be important to us all. In developing policy propositions for classroom debates, choose topics that are *current, controversial,* and *complex.* For a different way of practicing debate skills, you might try a *literary debate* or *historical debate.*

Activities

☐ Break into small groups. Have each member of your group bring a newspaper or magazine editorial to class. After all group members have read their editorials to the group, choose one topic and phrase it as a debate proposition.

☐ Have each group state its debate proposition to the rest of the class. The class can evaluate the phrasing of the debate proposition and its value as a topic for debate.

☐ The class can rank the debate propositions in the order in which they would prefer to debate them—after a spokesperson from each group has a chance to speak up for the group's choice.

GETTING AT THE ISSUES   7

How to analyze debate propositions

No matter which side of a debate you are on—affirmative or negative—there are a number of steps you must take in preparing your debate "case." The first of these is:

DEFINING TERMS

In everyday life, if you carefully define the terms you use, you may eliminate any need to argue. If you and your friend, for example, disagree about whether a certain school rule is fair, you may save yourselves a lot of grief if you first establish exactly what *fair* means to each of you. To you, *fair* may mean *how the majority of the students want to be treated.* To your friend, it may mean *all students should be treated in the same way.* Those are two different ideas. If you understand the difference between them and come up with a definition of *fair* that you both can accept, you may end up debating the question calmly instead of shouting at each other.

In the same way, if in a debate proposition you speak of "hair of reasonable length" or "an increase in allowance" you may be in trouble. It's better to establish right away that in this case "reasonable length" means down to the ear lobes for boys and to the waist for girls—or that "an increase in allowance" means a 20% increase. That way, everyone knows exactly what's being debated.

Prompt and precise definition of terms is essential to good analysis. In the last chapter we mentioned the proposition "Resolved: That the United States should establish a system of compulsory service by all citizens." What is meant by *compulsory service?* Military service? Alternate service? In this country or abroad? Who are "all citizens"? Men and women both? The way you and your fellow debaters define the proposition determines the kind of information you'll look for in preparing to debate. Your definition of terms also serves to limit the issues to be debated.

The main responsibility for defining terms in a debate actually lies with the affirmative side. In debate tournaments, the debate usually opens with a statement of definitions by the affirmative. The negative side, in its turn, indicates to what extent it accepts the affirmative's definitions.

In classroom debates it's a good idea for both sides to work together in advance to define terms. If you don't, the debate may become an argument over definitions instead of a debate over issues.

There are several ways to define the terms of a debate proposition. One way is to use some authority—a dictionary, encyclopedia, or leading text—in which there is a clear definition you can agree with. For instance, *Black's Law Dictionary* could be used in defining what is meant by "the jury system" in a proposition calling for a change in that system.

Another way to define terms is by *example.* If your proposition speaks of "a national program of public works," you could define that by saying "a public works program such as the one run by the Works Projects Administration in the 1930s."

You may define terms by *negation,* stressing what a term does *not* mean. If your proposition urges federal aid to private schools, you could say that by "private" you do not mean privately owned schools which are operated for profit.

There are other ways of shedding light on the terms of a debate proposition. You may delve into the *derivation*—the origin of a term. For instance, if the proposition is "Resolved: That the federal government should *establish,* finance, and administer programs to control air and water pollution in the United States," you may explain that the word *establish* is derived from the Latin *stabilis*—meaning firm, stable. To establish a program then is to create something with the idea of its being permanent and stable.

You may *compare* or *contrast* a difficult or technical term with one that is more familiar. If you are debating whether the next drama production is to be produced on a "raked" stage, you could define a raked stage by comparing it with a conventional stage. Whereas a stage is generally flat, a raked stage is one which is slanted at an angle.

Since most propositions contain several terms that must be defined, no single method mentioned is likely to work satisfactorily for defining all terms. Use whichever method or combination of methods works for each term you think needs defining.

☐ Divide into small groups and define the *italicized* terms in the following propositions. Discuss each one till you all agree on the definition. Then discuss your definitions with the rest of the class and try, as a class, to agree on a definition for each term.

☐ Resolved: That the federal government should ban the sale of all detergents containing *phosphates*.

☐ Resolved: That *environmental control standards* should be reduced.

☐ Resolved: That smoking in *public places* should be illegal.

☐ Resolved: That two credits in *practical arts* be required for high school graduation.

☐ Resolved: That Congress should prohibit *unilateral* United States *military intervention* in foreign countries.

INVESTIGATING THE DEBATE PROPOSITION

Just as most good lawyers do meticulous research into the facts of each case they present in court, so good debaters investigate and analyze each proposition.

Define the Problem

The first step in this kind of investigation is to define the problem (or problems). Whether you are debating values—"Resolved: That it is important for students to develop an appreciation of art"—or policy—"Resolved: That outstanding student works of art should be displayed throughout the school building," you are debating because someone thinks a *problem* exists. In the first instance someone sees a lack of art appreciation as a problem. In the second instance several problems—lack of student appreciation of art, a dull-looking school building, no pride in the school—have led someone to propose a particular solution.

When you have picked out the problem or problems, ask yourself the following questions:

How long have we had the problem?
What seems to have caused it?
What solutions, if any, have been tried before?
Why didn't they work?
In what ways are conditions different now?

Define the Controversy

Many times the answers to these questions will lead you right into the next step in investigation: *defining the controversy.* You can pin this down by asking still more questions:

Why are you debating this particular topic at this particular time?
What is causing you or others to be concerned about certain facts, or to question certain values, or to favor changing a particular policy?
What are the different views that people have of the positions?

For example, if you were debating the value of foreign language programs in your high school, you would begin your investigation by asking: What is going on right now in education or in the world that makes this topic controversial? Why are people interested in it? What is the nature of the controversy about it? Maybe some people believe that training in foreign languages isn't important any more because so many people in other countries speak English. Maybe others believe foreign language programs are too expensive. Still others may think foreign language programs are important in order to promote greater understanding among nations.

To find out what all the sides of the controversy are, you should look into the history of the controversy. In delving into the origins of a controversy, you discover still more of the arguments—both pro and con—that have been used before. While you may not want to use any of these arguments today, you will probably have gained insight into the reasons behind current opinion. You may find, for example, that your school once cut back its sports program in order to expand its foreign language department. That might explain why some people currently feel that "foreign language programs are too expensive." No matter whether you are on the affirmative or negative side of the debate, this information could be useful when building your case—or when pointing out the weaknesses in the other side's.

☐ Divide into small groups. Then
  1. Investigate a school or community problem. Define the problem and the controversy. Do this by interviewing people involved in the problem—or in efforts at solving it—and by reading any local news articles about the problem. After each member of the group has conducted an interview or read some articles, try to formulate group answers to the questions under defining the problem and defining the controversy. How could this information be used to build a case for taking a particular course of action?

  or

  2. Follow the same procedure as in the first activity, except use a state or national problem. Using such a problem may mean relying on articles and not interviews. Your task would still be to define the problem and the controversy.

STOCK ISSUES

Further investigation, particularly of policy propositions, may make use of *stock issues*. These are really not issues but instead are questions meant to reveal issues. The questions are so general they can be used with practically any debate topic. The traditional stock issue questions are:

1. *Is there a need for a change in the* status quo? Are there problems in the *status quo* (in the situation as it is now)? Are these problems serious enough to warrant a change? Can the problems be solved easily? Or are they *inherent* in the present system—so tied to it that the system itself must be changed in order to eliminate the problems?

2. *Will the affirmative plan solve the problems in the* status quo? Is the affirmative plan practical—will it work? It's not enough for the affirmative side to say something ought to be done—they must show how it can be done.

There is a difference between the debate *proposition* and the *affirmative plan.* The debate proposition is like an architect's drawing of what a house should look like from the outside when completed. The affirmative plan is like a blueprint that carefully outlines how the house is to be put together to look that way. The proposition may be "Resolved: That a year of a foreign language be required for high school graduation." The specific affirmative plan must deal with answering such questions as: What particular foreign language? How can we provide enough teachers? What equipment will be needed? Can it be financed? What other course, or courses, will have to be dropped by most students?

The affirmative plan then must show how the change stated in the debate proposition will be brought about and carried out.

3. *Is the affirmative plan the most desirable solution to the problem?* Is there a better way of taking care of the problems? Could the affirmative plan possibly introduce new and larger problems? Regardless of the side you'll be on, you should give some attention to this question. If you're on the negative side, you can use the "new and larger problems" as an effective argument. If you're on the affirmative side, you should first try to avoid the new problems—or if you can't, at least prepare arguments to support your contention that new benefits outweigh the "new and larger problems."

Specific Issues

By applying the above stock issue questions to your debate proposition, you can develop *specific issues*. To arrive at specific issues, substitute specific words from your debate proposition for the general stock issue terms *status quo* and *affirmative plan*. For example, let's say you were debating the resolution that "Political campaigns should be publicly financed." The stock issues and specific issues would line up this way:

Stock Issue	*Specific Issue*
1. Is there a need for a change in the *status quo?*	1. Is there a need for a change in the *present way of financing political campaigns?*
2. Will the *affirmative plan* solve the problems in the *status quo?*	2. Will the affirmative method of *publicly financing political campaigns* solve the problems in the *present way of financing political campaigns?*
3. Is the *affirmative plan* the most desirable solution to the problem?	3. Is the affirmative method of *publicly financing political campaigns* the most desirable solution to the problem?

It's in seeking to answer these questions that you begin your search for supportive materials that will build sound arguments and a sound case.

SUMMING UP

In analyzing a debate proposition, you might begin by defining the terms of the proposition. This way, you make sure that you debate important issues instead of shouting at one another.

You might define the terms of your proposition by quoting an *authority* or by using *examples*. Or you may define through *negation*, explaining what a term is not. *Derivation* is another means of defining—by explaining a term's origin and meaning. And finally you can *compare* and *contrast* a term with one that is familiar.

Analysis also requires careful investigation of the proposition to determine the nature of the problem and the reasons for the current controversy surrounding it. This investigation seeks to answer questions about such things as the history of the problem, any solutions that were tried before, and the various viewpoints currently held about the problem.

Further investigation makes use of three *stock issue* questions. (1) Is there a need for a change in the *status quo?* (2) Will the affirmative plan solve the problems in the *status quo?* (3) Is the affirmative plan the most desirable solution to the problem?

By rephrasing these questions so that they fit your debate proposition, making them *specific issues,* you are ready to begin your search for sound arguments and a sound case.

Activities

☐ Take the current national topic for high school debaters and investigate it on your own, using the questions below. Then go over the same questions in class. Are there any answers you as a class disagree on? Do any of the answers suggest that the affirmative side or the negative side might have the "easier," more convincing side of the debate? If so, which side—and why?
    a. Why do you think this particular topic was chosen for this particular year?
    b. What is the problem posed in the proposition?

c. How long has it been a problem?
d. What are some possible causes of the problem?
e. What solutions, if any, have been tried before?
f. Why didn't they work?
g. In what ways are conditions different now from when the previous solutions were tried?
h. What controversy surrounds the problem?
i. How did the controversy arise?

☐ Bring to class your definitions for the important terms in the following propositions:

(a) Resolved: That political campaigns should be publicly financed.
(b) Resolved: That the federal government should provide comprehensive medical care for all United States citizens.

Compare your definitions with others in class. Are there many significant differences? What are they? What might account for them? As a class, rework your definitions until you agree on them.

☐ What would be the specific issues if you were debating proposition (b) above?

☐ Take the current national topic—or one of the class's choosing—and debate the issue posed in stock issue number one (Is there a need for a change in the *status quo?*)

☐ For this activity the entire class should be divided in half—one half which thinks there *is* a serious need for a change and one half which thinks there *is not.* (Some students may have to end up on a side they don't really agree with. If that happens to you, remember that it's good training to be able to debate effectively on *either* side.)

☐   Hold a mini-debate (of no more than ten minutes) letting spokespeople for the affirmative side state what the *status quo* is, what the problem is, and why they think there's a need for a change. Then let the negative's spokespeople state, within the same time limit, their version of the *status quo,* why they think there's no great problem and no need for a change.

☐   Both sides should meet separately in advance to plan their arguments and choose their spokespeople. Afterwards, discuss as a class and with your teacher which side made the most effective presentation and why.

GETTING YOUR IDEAS TOGETHER

8

How to build sound arguments

Terms and problem defined? Proposition investigated and analyzed? Okay. Here's where you start building your argument—in support of the proposition if you're on the affirmative side, against the proposition if you're on the negative side. Either way, your first step will be to find and use *evidence*.

EVIDENCE

You need more than a loud voice to convince others that your side is right—you need some kind of supportive materials, or *evidence*. You may claim that your basketball team is the best in the state, but why should your cousin in another city believe you? But if you can cite a superior won-lost record, a comparative advantage in scores against common rivals, or (better yet) an actual victory over your cousin's team, you'll sound a lot more convincing. Your cousin may not believe you, but an objective judge probably will!

Argument is a special term in debate. It does not mean "arguing down." It doesn't mean a heated dispute. *Argument* means, in debate, a conclusion—and your reasons for that conclusion. These reasons must be supported by good evidence tied together in a logical way.

To support your argument, or position, you will need to locate and use the best evidence possible. To say only "Highway deaths seem to me to have gone down since the lowering of speed limits" is not enough. Suppose, though, that you back that up by citing a report by the commander of the state police showing a 35% reduction in accidents and fatalities. You will then have used evidence to support your opinion.

LOCATING EVIDENCE

For debate, you'll need the best evidence you can find, for it is going to have to be able to stand up under attack from the other side. Thorough, accurate research is crucial. As you would if you were preparing a speech, look for facts and opinions on both sides, use current materials, vary your sources, and record all information accurately.

Information obtained directly from experts may be helpful in analysis and in supporting your position. You can get such information through interviews and through letters.* (One caution, though—evidence obtained through interviews, partly because it is hard to check, is not always allowed in tournament debate.) A student preparing for a classroom debate on "Resolved: That Congress should outlaw the manufacture, sale, and possession of handguns" wrote for information from the Director of the FBI, the President of the National Rifle Association, his local chief of police, and the district commander of his state's highway patrol. Responses to his letters gave him added insight into the issue and information that he used to support his position in the debate.

Government documents are good sources of information for debates, especially since many debates center on government issues. To find out what documents might be helpful to you, consult the *Monthly Catalog of U.S. Government Publications,* which should be available in your library. This publication will let you know what government materials are available on your topic and where to write for them.

Another valuable source of information about the national high school debate proposition is the National University Extension Association. The N.U.E.A. puts out a helpful publication, *The Forensic Quarterly.*

---

* See *Investigating: Gathering Information,* by Jane Stine, in this series, for pointers on interviewing and on writing information-seeking letters.

One issue usually contains an analysis of the debate problem area and a reading list, while other issues have more general articles for high school debaters.

For most topics, however, you will need to rely heavily on what you find in your library's reference section, especially the *Readers' Guide to Periodical Literature* which can refer you to back issues of magazines, and the *Social Sciences and Humanities Index,* which will help you find specialized magazines on the topics that are listed in the subject index of your library's card catalogue. You should also check almanacs, encyclopedias, and back issues of newspapers.

PRE-TESTING EVIDENCE

In Chapter 2, in the public speaking section, five types of supportive materials were discussed: (1) examples, (2) visual aids, (3) testimony, (4) comparison, and (5) statistics. As a public speaker uses caution in choosing what materials to use, so a debater should check out—pre-test—every scrap of evidence before bothering to record it. Make sure you follow the suggestions mentioned earlier for examining supportive materials. Pre-test your evidence by asking such questions as:

Does it really have a bearing on your case?
Is it up-to-date?
Are the experts who are quoted truly experts in the field?
Is any statistical information based on representative sampling?
Is the information accurate?
Will your audience accept it as being supportive of your argument?

USING EVIDENCE

Even more important than having lots of pre-tested evidence is the ability to use that evidence properly. Any fact is open to different interpretations. For instance, suppose I asked you, "What's the highest mountain known?" Easy to answer? Not really. Actually there are several possible answers because of the way the question is phrased. Nix Olympica on Mars, for example, is estimated to be about 15 miles high. The tallest peak on this planet, measured from the earth's center, is a mountain in the Andes. There's still a catch—if you measure from surrounding land, instead of from the earth's center, Mauna Loa, which rises 30,000 feet, is highest, though the land around it is a sea bed. Most mountains, of course, are measured from sea level, so most people would answer Mount Everest—which is the highest mountain measured that way.

Debaters always need to guard against the tendency to use evidence carelessly, without regard for its true meaning. The statement "The highest mountain known is Mount Everest" is accurate only if you have defined exactly how the mountain was measured. If you quote a population statistic, you have to state as of what year the town, state, or country contained that number of people.

Be wary too of claiming that a bit of information or a fact says more than it really does. You may know that Sally made a 91 on the history exam while Cindy made an 85, but that's not conclusive proof that Sally is a better history student than Cindy. Cindy may normally score higher than Sally but for any number of reasons—illness, other homework, different style of test, extra effort on Sally's part—her score was lower on this one test. Guard against generalizing!

FUNKY WINKERBEAN   Tom Batiuk

☐ Review the discussion about *Selecting Supportive Materials* in Chapter 2.

☐ Bring a newspaper or magazine editorial to class. Be prepared to answer the following questions:
   a. What types of supportive materials—evidence—were used in the editorial?
   b. Does the evidence seem acceptable in light of the tests of evidence mentioned above?

c. How well is the evidence used? Does the editor claim more support for his or her viewpoint than the actual evidence seems to warrant? Or does the editor use evidence fairly and accurately, without claiming it proves more than it actually does?

☐ If possible interview a trial lawyer to find out how he or she uses evidence to build a case. Find out how the lawyer finds and pretests evidence. Could you apply any of those methods to debate? How?

Recording Evidence

Since you are not likely to remember everything you read in preparing for a debate, you need to develop a good system of note-taking. A good system of note-taking enables you to (1) organize your notes efficiently in order to build a case, (2) have evidence available during the actual debate to use in refuting an opponent's argument, (3) rebuild your own case during the debate with examples or testimonials, and (4) protect yourself, by the accuracy and thoroughness of your notes, against any challenges of being unethical or having a "faulty memory."

Note-taking, as you know if you've read *Investigating: Gathering Information,* by Jane Stine, in this series, can be a very personal kind of thing. No system is good if it doesn't work for you. But most debaters, since they have to use their notes while the debate is going on, find note cards to be the best place to record information. Cards can be shuffled and sorted. They are easier than sheets of paper to file and less bulky to handle during the debate. Most debaters find 3 x 5 cards too small, 5 x 8 cards too large, and thus compromise on 4 x 6.

It is usually best to put only one piece of information on each card and write on only one side of the card. Information is then easy to locate when you need to find it quickly to answer an opponent's challenge.

You may also wish to "color-code" your evidence to make it easier to spot. For instance, you might record affirmative information supporting the proposed change on blue cards. Information that the negative might use against the change you could record on yellow cards, and general evidence on white cards. This way you would have evidence for either side at your fingertips, in case you were called on to debate first one side and then the other—a common procedure in tournament debating.

Needless to say, information should be recorded as neatly and accurately as possible. Have you ever had trouble reading your own writing a month after you've written something in your notebook? If so, think of the problems your partner may have if you're on a two-person debate team and are sharing evidence cards. If your writing's particularly hard to read, you might consider printing or even typing.

One thing that is very hard to fight in a debate is a true accusation of inaccuracy. If your opponent can prove that something you say is inaccurate, not only will you lose points if the debate is being judged, but you'll lose credibility as well. Your opponents, the judges, and maybe even your own teammate will tend to doubt other statements you make.

You may wish to use some general note cards to guide you in the actual delivery of your debate speeches. Prepare and use these as you would if you were delivering a regular public speech. Make any fact you put down, either on a "speechmaking" card or a separate evidence card, as complete and exact as it can be. Check all statistics; it's easy to copy a number incorrectly. Record each quotation verbatim—exactly as it appears in the source—if possible. If a quote is too long to record verbatim, omit some of it, but be careful to indicate omissions by using ellipsis dots (. . .) and make sure the omission doesn't change the meaning. (You've seen those movie ads which say "Finest film. . . ." You've probably also heard jokes people sometimes make about what might have been left out: "Finest film for people who like to sleep at the movies."

To aid in gaining acceptance of a piece of evidence, you may wish to mention the source of your information. Record this information near the top of each card for quick reference. Bibliographic information should include: author, title of the publication, publisher, publication date, and page number(s). You can also add information about the author's qualifications and the nature of the organization publishing the material if that will be important for your argument.

At the very top of each card, you should write the subject heading—what the card is about—and if you haven't used colored cards also write "affirmative" or "negative" depending on which side's argument is supported by the information.

If you were arguing that financial support and public emphasis should be given to the Bicentennial Era (1976-1989), you might use an evidence card like the one shown on page 99.

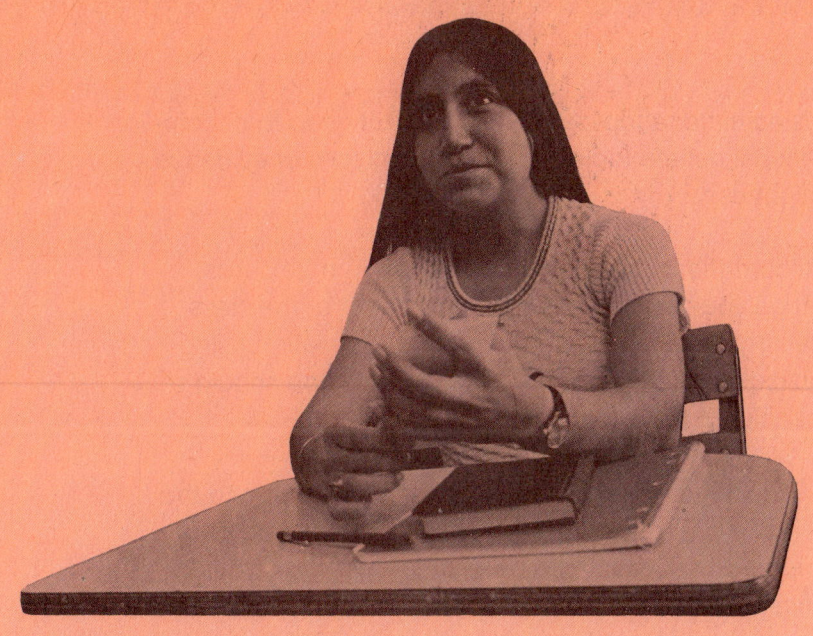

> 1. <u>Benefits of Bicentennial Era</u>   Affirmative 2.
> 3. John D. Rockefeller 3rd   Eldest of Rockefeller 4.
>   brothers. Interested in
>   Population problems and
>   Philanthropy
> 5. "Taking the Bicentennial Seriously," <u>Newsweek</u>
>   (April 1, 1974) pg. 11.
> 6. "If it is true that the ferment and uncertainty and
>   adversity of today are in many ways reminiscent of
>   the America of 200 years ago, then the Bicentennial
>   could be a providential opportunity. It could provide
>   a rallying ground for diverse points of view. It
>   could help generate the spirit of renewal and re-
>   dedication that we need so much."

Code for Card

1. **Subject heading**
2. **Side of the issue**
3. **Author**
4. **Author's qualifications**
5. **Bibliographical information**
6. **Exact quotation to be used**

☐ Using either a topic you've already chosen to debate—or the national debate topic—locate three pieces of evidence you might use.

☐ Record those pieces of information on note cards. Exchange your cards with another member of the class and see if your classmate can find the information using the bibliographic information on your card. You should also check out his or her cards.

☐ Divide into small groups. Take turns explaining to the members in your group how you would use one of your evidence cards. Group members may further test your evidence.

TYING IT TOGETHER—REASONING

The process by which you attempt to establish a relationship between your supporting material and your position in the debate is called *reasoning*. The two basic forms of reasoning, deductive and inductive, were explained in Section One of this book. You might want to go back to pp. 30-31 and review that explanation before trying the following activities.

☐ Work in small groups. Using *only* the information provided in each major premise and minor premise, see if your group can agree on a conclusion to each of the following syllogisms.

    a. Major Premise: Twentieth-century U.S. presidents have been either Republicans or Democrats.
       Minor Premise: Woodrow Wilson was a twentieth-century president.
       Conclusion: Therefore, _____.

    b. Major Premise: No city in Wyoming has more than 100,000 people.
       Minor Premise: Helena is not in Wyoming.
       Conclusion: Therefore, _____.

c. Major Premise: All changes are for the good.
   Minor Premise: The new law will be a change.
   Conclusion: Therefore, _____.
d. Major Premise: All states have two people in the United States Senate.
   Minor Premise: Kansas is a state.
   Conclusion: Therefore, _____.

☐ Have each group prepare a syllogism (complete with major premise, minor premise, and conclusion) that the rest of the class will accept as correct. Discuss each syllogism thoroughly, explaining why you do or do not accept it.

Inductive reasoning, as you'll remember, is the reverse of deductive reasoning. Even though you may ofen use inductive reasoning yourself, you probably realize that it can have flaws. For instance, in the example given in Section One, of the youngster who wants to go to camp, even though the six young people named may be going to camp, there may be many more in the class who are *not* going. The hypothesis that "everyone" is going may not stand up under close examination.

☐ Bring a newspaper or magazine editorial to class. Read it to the group you worked with on the syllogism activities. Explain whether you think the writer is trying to get the reader to reason deductively or inductively. Does the group agree with you? Can you reach an agreement?

Testing Inductive Reasoning

Inductive arguments may best be examined by asking questions about particular types of inductive reasoning. Four of the main types of inductive reasoning used are (1) reasoning by example, (2) reasoning by analogy, (3) sign reasoning, and (4) causal reasoning.

Reasoning by Example In this method, you use selected examples to support your main contention. You might claim that the American League is superior to the National League and point to (1) the results of the World Series between 1920-1960 and (2) the ease with which certain players have improved their records when traded from the American League to the National League. Under each of these headings you will point to specific examples—scores under (1) and players under (2).

Reasoning by example may be tested by asking five questions:
1. Are there a reasonable number of examples?
   If 120 baseball players have been traded from American League teams, and you are only pointing to two successful ones, then you hardly seem to be using a significant number of examples.
2. Are the examples typical?
   Davey Johnson may have been successful when he moved from Baltimore to Atlanta, but is his success typical? Is such success enjoyed by more than 50% of those who make a transfer?
3. Do the examples cover the critical period of time being discussed?
   If you're debating which league is best today, the World Series results from 1920-1960 don't have much to do with what you're trying to prove.
4. Are there enough negative examples to seriously damage your contention?
   Are there many players who were traded from National League teams to American League teams and enjoyed great success? Are there many American League players who flopped when traded to the National League?
5. Are the examples relevant?
   Do the examples used—if they pass all the other tests—really serve to demonstrate your contention?

When you are testing reasoning by example, you should be able to answer *yes* to questions 1, 2, 3, and 5, and *no* to question 4. If you can't, you're in trouble—or your opponent is, if it's your opponent's reasoning you're testing.

Reasoning by Analogy This is a type of reasoning based on comparisons of similar places, people, objects, or events. You may reason that since two people are alike in terms of certain things you know about them, they must be alike in other ways.

An Oklahoma legislator, for example, might contend that since a particular tax structure was working well for Texas, it should work well for Oklahoma. He might claim that the two states are alike since they border on one another and since oil and cattle have contributed to the wealth of both.

You would test such reasoning by asking the following questions:
1. Are there significant points of similarity?
    Are the states equal in population? Do they have similar financial needs? Are sources of state income and distribution of wealth similar?
2. Are the differences crucial enough to destroy the analogy?
    In other words, if the answer to any of the questions you ask under number one is *no*, then the analogy is seriously weakened. If the answer to all questions is *no*, the analogy is probably false.

The analogy, although it is often vivid and memorable, is seldom very sound proof.

Reasoning from Sign You probably use sign reasoning often. Your math teacher walks into class dressed in a suit and tie, and you brace yourself for an hour of hard work. Another day he walks in with an open collar and colorful sweater, and class members prepare for a more informal class period. His different ways of dressing probably don't *cause* a difference in the way he conducts class, but you may have learned to read the differences as *signs*, or indications, that his teaching styles will vary.

Sign reasoning should be tested by asking:
1. Is the sign related to the anticipated state or action?
    Can differences in clothes really relate to behavior patterns? Again, is this an accidental—occasional—sign or is it typical?
2. Are there other signs which may be even more accurate predictors?
    The day of the week may be a better sign if your teacher's free periods precede your class on Tuesdays and Thursdays while he has supervisory duties on Mondays, Wednesdays, and Fridays.

Causal Reasoning In using causal reasoning people assert that one thing (cause) produces another (effect). If you take a known course of action (hitting another student in the face with a lemon pie as a part of a comedy act), we can predict the effect (audience laughter). Political commentators sometimes observe that a leading politician has made certain remarks (cause) and confidently predict the defeat of a particular bill (effect).

You can also argue from effect to cause. The political commentator may note that a bill has been defeated in committee (effect) and from that infer that the chairman opposed the bill (cause).

To test causal reasoning you should ask:

1. Is the alleged cause capable of producing the effect?

   Can one person's opposition kill a bill in Congress?
   Can breaking a mirror really cause bad luck?

2. Is the alleged cause the only factor that could account for the effect?

   Highway fatalities dropped significantly when speed limits were lowered during the energy crisis in the 1970s, but people have also pointed to other factors—scarcity of gas, closing of stations—as contributing to the reduction of fatalities.

3. Is the alleged cause capable of producing other, and undesirable, effects?

   You may urge a continuation of low speed limits (cause) to keep down highway fatalities (desirable effect) but your opponents may contend that low speed limits (cause) result in shipping delays that hurt the economy (undesirable effect).

☐ Read a mystery novel or watch a detective show on television and then explain to the class the reasoning processes used to solve the crime.

☐ Write a letter to a newspaper editor, in which you support or oppose a recent or pending government decision. Read the letter aloud in class and have class members "test" your reasoning.

☐ Find examples—in newspapers, magazines, speeches, ordinary conversations—of each of the types of reasoning mentioned in this chapter. Discuss in class the results of your search. Do some types of reasoning seem to be used more frequently than others? If so why might this be?

AVOIDING AND ATTACKING FALLACIES

Fallacies are errors in reasoning. There are many different kinds of fallacies, but those listed below—the "slovenly seven"—seem to occur most frequently. Try to avoid them in building your own arguments and also try to expose them when your opponents use them.

Avoiding the Slovenly Seven

The slovenly seven fallacies are: (1) *Ad Hominem* attacks, (2) Begging the Question, (3) Centimeter-Kilometer, (4) Either-Or, (5) False Analogy, (6) False Cause, and (7) Hasty Generalization.

Ad Hominem *Ad hominem* arguments attack the person rather than the argument. Some religious leaders of long ago used this type of argument against Jesus. They asked "What good can come out of Nazareth?" The implication was that no man's ideas could be good if that man were from Nazareth. If a debater tries to disprove an opponent's argument on the grounds that the opponent is of a particular nationality, political party, religion, or race then he or she is using an *ad hominem* attack.

Begging the Question This is acting as if an argument is true when, in fact, it is the very question at issue. If a senator debating a bill said, "This bill should be defeated because it shouldn't be passed," the senator would not have proved a thing. The argument the senator was using (it shouldn't be passed) was the same thing as the question at issue (whether it should be defeated).

Centimeter-Kilometer Give them a centimeter and they'll take a kilometer. This fallacy consists of the idea that to allow a certain action will inevitably lead to more serious consequences—when that is not necessarily true. A teacher may be guilty of this fallacy when he or she refuses to accept a late assignment "because then you'll always be coming up with excuses to turn your work in late." Debaters may be guilty of the fallacy when they urge defeat of a proposition "because once the federal government starts a small program they'll soon be running the whole show."

Either-Or Fallacy An either-or fallacy occurs when someone oversimplifies a problem and improperly reduces the number of alternatives to two. You no doubt have been exposed to people who said things like, "Either you agree with me or you're not my friend." In the same way, debaters may say, "Either you support my plan or you're obviously against progress." The tendency here is to see one side as right and one side as wrong—and not even realize there may be more than two sides.

False Analogy A false analogy occurs when someone compares two things that are essentially unlike. For example, someone might argue that "to propose making smoking in public places illegal is as ridiculous as proposing a law against public gum chewing." While both may be viewed by some people as "tasteless habits" and therefore alike in that sense, they are dissimilar in many important ways. The threat of smoke to the health of others is the main reason for proposals against smoking in public. Gum chewing is no threat—so the analogy is false.

False Cause The fallacy of the false cause occurs when you label something as the cause of something else on insufficient evidence. The false assumption here is that an event that happens first is necessarily the cause of an event that happens later.

For example, some fans pointed out that under Vince Lombardi the Green Bay Packers were the most successful team in pro football, but following his departure they collapsed. The cause of the collapse? Those fans said it was Lombardi's leaving. Actually, certain players also left, and others were injured about the same time, so there is not sufficient evidence to establish that Lombardi's leaving was the sole cause of the collapse.

Hasty Generalization A hasty generalization is a statement or argument based on an insufficient numbers of examples. Those guilty of this fallacy include those who: (1) read of one politician's criminal conduct while in office and then label all politicians as crooks or (2) read of one teenager's being arrested for drunken driving and start yelling about "what our youth are coming to." One or two individuals obviously don't represent an entire group. Still, some debaters try to build a case on just such limited examples.

☐ Look for examples of the "Slovenly Seven" and bring them to class. They should be surprisingly easy to find. Look at magazine articles and editorials, newspaper and television editorials, television and magazine advertisements. Listen to conversations, speeches, press conferences. Discuss your findings with your classmates.

☐ Keep a close check on your own reasoning for a period of time. Do you find yourself guilty of any of the "Slovenly Seven"? Some, more than others? If you think it will help, write down your uses of fallacious reasoning. Make a conscious effort to sharpen your reasoning in the future.

ATTACKING FALLACIES—REFUTATION

Refutation is the process of attacking your opponent's arguments. Each side is constantly trying to attack the other side's arguments while building up its own. During a debate, then, regardless of which side you are on, you would listen carefully to the opposing arguments and then, when it's your turn to speak, attack any of the following errors:

1. Fallacious reasoning—use of the "Slovenly Seven."
2. Errors in reasoning—reasoning that does not meet sound standards of argument. For example, a syllogism based on a false premise; a conclusion drawn from an irrelevant example or from a false analogy, sign, or cause.
3. Inconsistent statements—for example, a governor who says education is at the top of his or her "priority list" and later in the speech announces that actual funds for education will be cut in the coming year.
4. Evidence that does not meet the tests of good evidence.
5. Lack of sufficient evidence.

Debaters generally follow a certain pattern of refutation. This pattern involves five basic steps:

1. Restate your opponent's arguments as clearly and concisely as possible. It is very important, then, to listen well during the debate and to take accurate notes. You should always try to quote your opponent as exactly as possible. If you don't, he or she will probably point that out and claim that your argument is therefore faulty.

2. Show the significance of your opponent's argument to his or her position. In other words, show what will happen to your opponent's case if you demonstrate that his or her argument is not sound.

3. State concisely your objections to your opponent's argument. State any errors that have been made.

4. Introduce new evidence or reasoning to support your objections.

5. Summarize your refutation, being sure to emphasize the effect of the refutation on your opponent's case.

A sample of such a pattern of refutation—based on a particular argument—follows:

Opponent's Argument I would support my contention that we don't need this new road program by using a quote from Representative Goatbeard. In a 1960 speech, he pointed out, "There are plenty of miles of well-paved roads in this state. If we build any more new roads, every farmer in the state will want a paved road up to his door."

Refutation
1. My opponent has said, "We don't need this new road program."
2. My opponent rests the negative argument solely on the idea that there is no need for the new program. The negative side has not denied that money is available for new roads—that there is desire for them—nor that our state is capable of building them under this plan. Therefore, if we can demonstrate that a need does indeed exist—the negative argument and case falls.
3. My opponent's argument was based on a statement
    a. made by a man who lived in a district with well-paved roads, but who had not traveled in the northern part of our state where the new road is to be built.
    b. that is obviously out of date—road conditions have changed noticeably since 1960 and there certainly is need for new ones today.
    c. that is guilty of the centimeter-kilometer fallacy which suggests that just because this one new road is being requested we will be paving every farmer's "road up to his door."
4. My opponent has ignored a survey completed this year by the state highway department which describes Highway 52 as "in deplorable condition making it a virtual deathtrap."

5. I have shown you that

   a. my opponent's position rests solely on the denial of need.
   b. that his support of that position is based on out-of-date testimony from a man not familiar with the current problem and guilty of fallacious reasoning.
   c. that there is current, reliable information supporting the argument that there is a need for the new road program.
   My opponent's argument has fallen. Therefore, I ask you to vote for the affirmative proposal to build a new road in the northern part of our state to replace Highway 52.

☐ Find a newspaper or magazine editorial that has examples of several or all of the fallacies discussed in this chapter. Then, working with a small group of classmates, present your editorial. Have the members of your group refute your editorial. The refutation should follow the five basic steps outlined above. Did your group find all the fallacies you did? Did they find different ones?

SUMMING UP

By now you realize the importance of discovering and using sound evidence. Sound evidence, pre-tested by you, is essential to the development of a sound argument. Useful evidence should be recorded accurately on 4 x 6 note cards for use during the debate. In addition to writing down the piece of evidence you need, jot down information about the source and author of the information. This bibliographic information helps give credibility to your evidence.

As you gather good evidence, you begin the process of tying it together—reasoning. There are two basic forms of reasoning: deductive and inductive. Check a deductive argument for the truth of its premises and to see if the conclusion "follows" from the premises. Inductive reasoning is best tested by asking specific questions about each of the four main types of inductive reasoning—reasoning by example, reasoning by analogy, sign reasoning, and causal reasoning.

As a debater, you need to avoid fallacies, errors in reasoning. Those that seem to occur more frequently, the "Slovenly Seven," are:

Ad Hominem attacks

Begging the Question

Centimeter-Kilometer

Either-Or

False Analogy

False Cause

Hasty Generalization

In debate, of course, you not only seek to avoid making mistakes—you also seek to expose weaknesses in your opponent's arguments. The process by which you point out such weaknesses is called refutation. Refutation involves

restating your opponent's arguments

showing what will happen to the opposing case if the argument is shown to be unsound

pointing out your objections to the opposing argument

introducing new evidence or reasoning to support your objections

summarizing your refutation and emphasizing the effect of your refutation on your opponent's case.

Activities

☐ Interview a member of your state legislature, city council, or other local government body about a current state or local issue. Find out this person's position on the issue and his or her reasons for that position. Is the position based on careful reasoning? What kinds of reasoning? Is the reasoning based on sound evidence? What kinds of evidence?

☐ Later, divide into small groups and discuss how you would seek to refute the person's position. What kind of evidence would you look for? Where would you look for it? Try to use—as a group—the five basic steps of refutation to point out some weakness in the person's argument.

The Debate Itself   9

How to present your point of view

The formal statement, development, and proof of your point of view is referred to as a *case*. The affirmative's case consists of arguments and evidence designed to support the contention that a particular change is needed. Whatever the plan of attack of the affirmative side, it must support the debate proposition. The negative's case consists of arguments and evidence designed to support the contention that a particular change is *not* needed. Whatever strategy the negative side adopts, it must oppose the debate proposition.

The affirmative, because it must support the proposition, has the burden of proving that a change is needed. This requires that it develop a *prima facie* case. In debate, a *prima facie* case is one that casts enough doubt on the *status quo* to force the negative to respond to the affirmative arguments. A *prima facie* case in debate is much like a grand jury indictment. The indictment does not establish guilt, but it states that there is evidence enough to suggest that the possibility of guilt exists. The trial is then held and the issues debated fully. In a debate, the *prima facie* case does not establish a defeat for the negative, but it points out that there are enough things wrong with the *status quo* so that issues should be debated.

Once the affirmative side has established such a case, the negative has the burden of responding to the case through refutation. Both sides must respond to one another's arguments throughout the debate, but the affirmative retains the burden of winning acceptance for the proposition.

AFFIRMATIVE STRATEGIES

There are two basic strategies—two kinds of cases—that most affirmative speakers use to support their plan for a change. Those are (1) the needs case and (2) the comparative advantages case.

NEEDS CASE

A *needs case* is based on the idea that the *status quo* needs to be changed. An affirmative debater developing a needs case must point out: (1) that there are serious problems, or needs, inherent in the *status quo,* (By inherent, we mean some quality which exists in something and cannot be separated from it. Death and taxes are problems inherent in the human condition.) and (2) that the present system must be changed in order to eliminate, or reduce, the serious problems. The affirmative must also (3) develop a plan that is practical and will meet the needs for change, and (4) prove that the affirmative plan is the best possible way to solve the problems.

A recent classroom debate on the proposition, "Resolved: That the United States should adopt some form of parliamentary government" was debated on a needs basis. The affirmative side sought to establish first of all that there are serious enough problems in our present form of government to create the need for a change. The affirmative contended that the Executive branch is not responsive to the people and tends to assume too much power. After supporting this contention with specific examples, the affirmative argued that this lack of responsiveness was inherent in the present system. The contention there was that the people could do nothing about decisions they disliked because inherent in our system is a President locked in to a four-year term of office no matter what policies are set. The plan to remedy this inherent problem was a proposal to have a President elected by the majority of the representatives in Congress. This President would serve five years, or until his party lost a major vote in Congress. After describing how this plan would work, the affirmative then sought to show that it was the best solution.

Comparative Advantages

A *comparative advantages case* also seeks to change the present way of doing things to the way suggested by the affirmative. However, in a comparative advantages debate, disagreement centers not so much on goals as on whose *method* of attaining those goals offers the most advantages. The affirmative using a comparative advantages case stresses the advantages of his or her plan over the way things are currently being done. The affirmative emphasizes that the new plan will be *better* than the old way because of certain new and significant advantages.

For instance, everyone in a state legislative body may agree that the state should obtain money to build a new highway. The question is whether a new plan—toll roads—to raise money is really superior to the way money has been raised traditionally—higher taxes on state residents. Does the new plan promise to raise a significantly greater amount of money? Is the new plan a better way to increase the amount raised? Is it fairer? Quicker? Are there any significant disadvantages—changes in the state's image, or less interstate traffic, for instance—that might result from the plan? Can the advocates of the plan show that it really will work?

The steps in presenting the two affirmative approaches follow. The strategies are placed side by side so you may compare them.

Goal: Adopt the Affirmative Plan

Needs Case	Comparative Advantages
1. Establish idea of serious, inherent problems that create a need to change	(No reason to discuss need because there is general agreement on the goal to be reached—the disagreement is on the better method to reach that goal)
2. Present the plan	1. Present the plan
	2. Show how plan is different from *status quo*
3. Show how plan meets needs	3. Show plan to yield significant advantages over *status quo*
4. Show that plan is best workable solution to problem	4. Show that plan will work and actually yield advantages

☐ Discuss, in small groups, which affirmative strategy you think is better for this year's national high school debate topic. Why? Then select a spokesperson for your group who will state—and defend—your group's choice to the rest of the class.

☐ Following the same procedure as above (and consulting the chart on page 115 if you need to), discuss:
Resolved: That smoking in public places should be illegal.
Resolved: That the federal government should establish, finance, and administer programs to control air and water pollution in the United States.

Sometimes, although it is easy to show that there are problems—needs—in the *status quo,* it is not easy to prove that those needs are inherent. Under those circumstances, debaters sometimes combine needs case strategy with the strategies of the comparative advantages case, and end up with a modified comparative advantages case. However, while you are new at debate, you may find it to your advantage to concentrate on the needs and comparative advantages cases, at least until you have mastered both thoroughly.

NEGATIVE STRATEGIES

The purpose of the negative is to refute the affirmative's position. There are several methods the negative may choose. They are (1) defense of the *status quo,* (2) total refutation of the affirmative plan, (3) a minor repairs case, and (4) a counterplan. *No matter which approach the negative side adopts it must clash directly with the arguments of the affirmative side.*

In arguing against the change proposed by the affirmative, the negative could be said to favor the *status quo.* But since the burden of proof is on the affirmative side, the negative's job is primarily to break down the affirmative's argument. Thus the choice of negative strategies will always depend in part on the arguments the affirmative uses, and in part on the way the negative interprets the *status quo.*

DEFENSE OF THE *Status Quo*

A negative side defending the *status quo* is saying that there is no need to change. Using this strategy you would contend that the present system is working adequately. The stress would be on what is good about the present system. You would try to show that no serious, inherent problem exists under the present system. The political party in power usually defends the *status quo* in any election campaign debate. The "in" party contends that things are fine and will continue to improve if things are just left as they are. The choice of this strategy is usually made when you can strongly defend the present system, or see any alternatives as obviously worse.

TOTAL REFUTATION OF THE AFFIRMATIVE PLAN

If the affirmative case is particularly weak, you might use the second negative approach—total refutation of the affirmative plan. This plan is often used with the first plan—defense of the *status quo*. Any strategy—affirmative or negative—will involve some refutation, but total refutation focuses exclusively on tearing down opposing arguments without putting forth counter arguments. This approach should not be your only pre-planned debate strategy because it is likely to be successful only when your opposition is weak.

You can try to refute an affirmative plan on the grounds that it will not work because it is structurally unsound. Using the earlier example of financing a new highway by making it a toll road, the negative might contend that the proposed new route and the placement of the toll booths just don't make sense.

You might refute the plan on the grounds that, even if it were workable, it would not meet the needs the affirmative described. You could argue that it would be impossible to collect enough money from such a system to pay for the new road before it needed repair.

Finally, you may contend that the disadvantages created by the affirmative plan far outweigh the advantages. The negative could contend that trucks and other commercial traffic would avoid the toll road and thus cost the state needed business and revenue.

MINOR REPAIRS CASE

You may use a minor repairs case when you believe you must admit to certain weaknesses in the *status quo*, but still think they can be cured without a major change such as the one advocated by the affirmative. I own an old car that has difficulty starting on cold, damp days. An aggressive affirmative (with the burden of proof) car salesman is urging me to buy a new car. As the negative in this debate, I'm hard pressed to deny weaknesses in the current system (car). I can, however, argue that with some minor mechanical adjustments it will be almost as good as new. These minor repairs would certainly be less costly than the affirmative's proposal and thus more advantageous.

COUNTERPLAN

A fourth alternative available to the negative side is the counterplan. A counterplan is usually a surprise tactic. It is risky though, for it takes the burden of proof off the affirmative and places it on the shoulders of the negative. This means you have to be prepared to prove your solution is better than the affirmative's instead of just showing that the affirmative's is not good.

You can use a counterplan if you agree with the needs cited by the affirmative. First you admit you agree that the *status quo* needs changing—but then you contend that the affirmative plan is not workable, or that it is not the best answer to the problem. The best answer? Why, of course, it's your plan!

For instance, the negative debating

> Resolved: That the federal government should support parochial secondary and elementary schools

could agree with affirmative needs—parochial schools provide an important service and need financial help—while saying that federal support is not the best answer. As a counterplan, the negative can urge a plan for *state* support—as opposed to *federal* support which the affirmative must uphold.

☐ In small groups, discuss which negative strategy you think is best for this year's national debate topic and your reasons for thinking so. Then select a spokesperson for your group who will state—and defend—your group's choice to the rest of the class.

☐ Find an affirmative speech—one advocating a change—in *Vital Speeches, Congressional Digest,* or another source of contemporary speeches. Read to your group an outline

of the affirmative proposal you selected and let the rest of the group work out the negative strategy that would most effectively deal with the affirmative proposal. Take turns until each member of the group has read the outline he or she selected.

DEBATE FORMATS

There are several formalized structures for presenting your viewpoints. Which format you use will depend on your situation—your goals, the ease with which people can work together as teams, and the amount of time you have in a class period.

TRADITIONAL DEBATE FORMAT

Traditional debate format involves two speakers on each side, and two kinds of speeches: constructive and rebuttal. In the course of the debate, each speaker will deliver one constructive speech and one rebuttal speech.

The four constructive speeches are delivered first. The constructive speeches are used to state and develop each side's case. Although each speaker—except the first one—uses some refutation, the prime objective of constructive speeches is to establish the issues of the debate.

The second set of four speeches form the rebuttals. The purposes of each rebuttal speech are to (1) refute your opponent's arguments and (2) rebuild your own. No new issues are to be introduced during the rebuttal period, though you are free to use new evidence to support previously introduced arguments.

The first and last speakers are believed to gain an advantage from their speaking position. Because it is considered more difficult to prove a need for change than to support the *status quo,* the affirmative team is allowed to have the advantage of beginning and ending the debate; this somewhat offsets their burden of proof.

Speeches in debates usually have definite time limits maintained by a time keeper. Time limits for classroom debates are usually shorter than for tournaments since few schools have class periods longer than an hour. The order of speaking and time limits for the speeches follow:

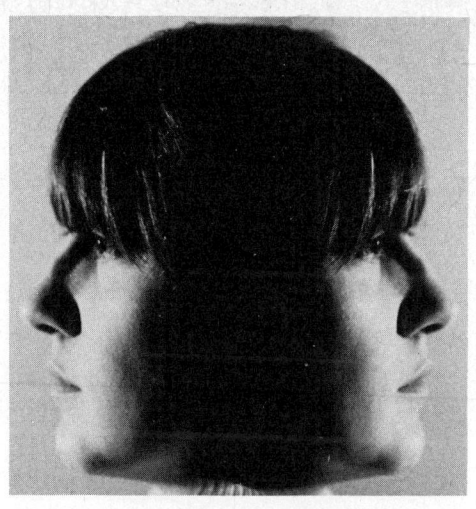

Traditional Debate Format

Speaking order	Tournament Time Limit	Suggested Classroom Time Limit
First Affirmative Constructive	10 minutes	6 minutes
First Negative Constructive	10 minutes	6 minutes
Second Affirmative Constructive	10 minutes	6 minutes
Second Negative Constructive	10 minutes	6 minutes
First Negative Rebuttal	5 minutes	3 minutes
First Affirmative Rebuttal	5 minutes	3 minutes
Second Negative Rebuttal	5 minutes	3 minutes
Second Affirmative Rebuttal	5 minutes	3 minutes

A Two-Person Debate

Often because of the number of people in a class or the nature of a particular debate topic, a debate will be scheduled with one affirmative speaker and one negative speaker. The format is similar to traditional debate, but it's simplified to fit the situation. The pattern is usually as follows: affirmative constructive (7 minutes), negative constructive and rebuttal (10 minutes), and affirmative rebuttal (3 minutes).

The Cross-Examination Debate

Up until the eighteenth century, witnesses in court cases were directly questioned only by the attorney who called them to prove a particular point in his case. Witnesses could not be questioned by the opposing side, that is, they could not be cross-examined. Today as you've no doubt observed on television, trial lawyers use the cross-examination of witnesses as one of their most important weapons.

The right to cross-examine an opposing debater was added to the standard debate format in the 1920s. Cross-examination is now the pattern used by most high schools, particularly those affiliated with the National Forensic League, the high school forensics honor society, which sponsors many speaking activities. A pattern for cross-examination follows:

Speaking Order	Tournament Maximum Time	Suggested Class Time
First Affirmative Constructive	8 minutes	5 minutes
First Affirmative is questioned by a Negative Speaker	3 minutes	2 minutes
First Negative Constructive	8 minutes	5 minutes
First Negative is questioned by an Affirmative Speaker	3 minutes	2 minutes
Second Affirmative Constructive	8 minutes	5 minutes
Second Affirmative is questioned by the *other* Negative Speaker	3 minutes	2 minutes
Second Negative Constructive	8 minutes	5 minutes
Second Negative is questioned by the *other* Affirmative Speaker	3 minutes	2 minutes
First Negative Rebuttal	4 minutes	3 minutes
First Affirmative Rebuttal	4 minutes	3 minutes
Second Negative Rebuttal	4 minutes	3 minutes
Second Affirmative Rebuttal	4 minutes	3 minutes

The cross-examination should be used *to clarify* positions and arguments in order to improve the quality of the debate. The examiner should also attempt *to expose any errors* in his or her opponent's analysis, reasoning, or evidence. If you obtain any significant information or admissions during the cross-examination you should use them in later speeches to help support your side's arguments.

When it is time for a cross-examination period to begin, the examiner (questioner) stands and moves toward the speaker. The examiner stands where he or she can look the speaker in the face and keep an eye on the audience and timekeeper. During a cross-examination period, the examiner is in complete charge—asking whatever questions seem appropriate and cutting off answers as he or she thinks best.

As an examiner you should make sure that each question contains only one point. Remember that your main function is to examine—not to make another constructive speech. Only ask questions that grow out of arguments that have already been used in the debate. Try not to permit the speaker to evade the issue. Finally, don't launch a personal attack against the speaker.

An example of a cross-examination period follows:

SPEAKER: I'm ready now for cross-examination.
EXAMINER: Thank you. You stated there is no need for a new highway program. Correct?
SPEAKER: Correct.
EXAMINER: You based that on an opinion by former Representative Goatbeard. What county did he represent?
SPEAKER: McCurtain.
EXAMINER: That's over 300 miles from any point on the proposed new highway. To your knowledge, did he ever visit the northern part of the state?
SPEAKER: Well, I'm not sure . . . it depends. . . .
EXAMINER: To your knowledge . . .
SPEAKER: To my knowledge, no.
EXAMINER: Your reference was to a rather dated 1960 speech. Are you aware of the report—just out this year—by the state highway department labeling old 52 "in deplorable condition—a virtual deathtrap"? Are you aware of that study?
SPEAKER: I've heard of it, but I haven't had a chance to read it yet.

As a witness you should answer questions, not ask them. Be as direct and fair in your answers as possible. If you don't know an answer, say so and let the judge(s) decide if you should have been prepared to answer it. Be brief, but feel free to qualify your answers when needed. Don't bother answering trick questions, and avoid personal arguments with the examiner. If you and your case are well prepared, you won't have to worry about exposing any serious weaknesses during cross-examination.

A Feedback Format

Inventive teachers and debate coaches have come up with other formats over the years. Particular rules and procedures vary on these as the circumstances dictate. Many students have found the feedback format to be an enjoyable change and educational.

In this, the debaters follow the same format as they do in traditional debate. However, the classroom is divided in half—with half the chairs on one side, half on the other, with a wide center aisle. Students favoring the affirmative sit on the speaker's right and those favoring the negative sit on the left. You as an audience member are free to move during the speech from one side to the other when a debater says something that changes your mind.

"Victory" is awarded to the team with the most audience members sitting on its side of the room at the conclusion of the debate. Seeing people actively registering their opinions forces debaters to use all they know about adjusting to audience feedback. Thus, speakers are not quite as formal or logical, but may display more real understanding of issues in order to constantly relate them to their "ever-voting" audience members.

THE DEBATE SPEECH

A debate speech, regardless of the format of the debate itself, is both persuasive and informative. You try to persuade listeners that your conclusion is correct and present enough information so that they will accept it. Remember, though, that the purpose of debate is not to see how much you can say in 6–10 minutes but to help others test two different conclusions—one advocated by the affirmative and the other by the negative. Time is of course a vital factor, but you shouldn't talk so fast that others can't understand you. You will have to be especially careful to state all your points clearly and concisely; there will be little time for the anecdotes and pleasantries that you might use in many public speaking situations.

Since all debaters—after the first affirmative speaker—are expected to clash with the ideas of the other side, debate speeches are delivered extemporaneously. Your ability to adapt—to think on your feet—can be improved through practice sessions. Get together with your partner (or a classmate, if you aren't debating in teams) and have him or her say a few things the other side might say and then get up and give your speech. After your partner critiques your speech, reverse the process and let him or her practice.

Speaker Duties

In any team situation, there is a division of labor. Working with a partner in debate is a bit like doubles in tennis in that respect; each member of the team has his or her own responsibilities. Two-person debate, on the other hand, is more like singles in tennis—each individual carries his or her side alone.

In any team debate, speaker responsibilities are usually shared along the following lines.

First Affirmative Constructive

The first affirmative speaker is responsible for stating the proposition, defining the terms of the proposition, and providing any needed historical background. If the affirmative team uses a needs case, the first affirmative usually presents the need for a change and outlines the affirmative plan. If the affirmative uses a comparative advantages case, the first affirmative presents the plan and cites one or two advantages of the plan over the *status quo*.

First Negative Constructive

The first negative accepts, rejects, or offers changes in the definitions provided by the first affirmative. He or she seeks to refute early affirmative arguments and advances the negative philosophy in this debate. The benefits of the present system are emphasized if the *status quo* is being defended. Any minor changes in the *status quo* should be explained if a minor repairs case is being used. If the negative is going to use a counterplan, it should be presented by the first negative speaker.

Second Affirmative Constructive

The second affirmative tries to refute any important arguments advanced by the first negative. If a needs case is being used, the second affirmative develops the plan and shows how it meets the needs cited by the first affirmative. If a comparative advantages case is being used, the second affirmative presents additional advantages and points out how they will come about only with the adoption of the affirmative plan. The affirmative case is summarized with an emphasis on the issues that have evolved.

Second Negative Constructive

The second negative seeks to refute all further affirmative arguments and advance any remaining issues in the negative case. He or she concludes with a summary of the issues of the debate with particular emphasis on the failure of the affirmative to carry out the burden of proof.

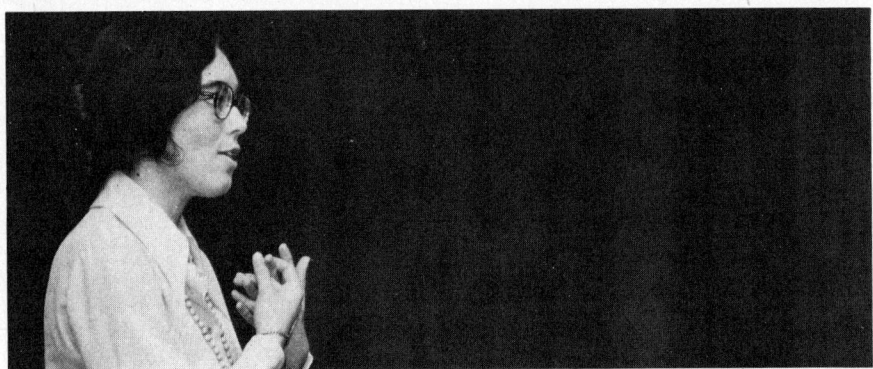

First Negative Rebuttal

The first negative speaker refutes the needs claimed by the affirmative if the needs case is being used, or the advantages claimed if the affirmative is using a comparative advantages case. Time is also spent re-emphasizing the positive points of the negative position.

First Affirmative Rebuttal

The first affirmative tries to counter any major negative objections and to rebuild the affirmative plan. New evidence to support the affirmative plan may be introduced.

Second Negative Rebuttal

The second negative's rebuttal is used to re-emphasize the weaknesses of the affirmative case, to rebuild and summarize the negative position, and to request a vote for the negative team.

SECOND AFFIRMATIVE REBUTTAL

The most important summary is that made by the second affirmative at the end of the rebuttal speech—the final speech in the entire debate. This last rebuttal should include refutation of any remaining key negative arguments and a summary favorable to the affirmative position, in order to get a favorable vote from the judge or audience.

JUDGING AND BEING JUDGED

After a debate, you might simply let people vote for the side they think is right. That's the way it's done at school board meetings and in Congress. However, in a classroom or in a tournament, it doesn't seem fair to penalize someone who has done a great job of presenting the unpopular side of an issue. This is especially true since individuals aren't always free to debate an issue or a side to which they're committed. To promote learning and improve the fairness of the decision, ballots are used for tournament debates and many classroom debates. Judges—especially ones chosen to judge in tournaments, probably your teacher and fellow students in the classroom—are asked to vote for the team that does the *best job of debating*—regardless of which team they agree with.

In judging, remember that the affirmative side has the burden of proof—it must show a need to change and develop a plan that meets that need, or at least present a plan that will do things better than the *status quo*. The negative side has the burden of rebuttal—it must refute the affirmative plan and build a case for the negative position.

In addition to deciding which side deserves a decision, judges usually evaluate each speaker. These evaluations help each speaker see where he or she was strong or weak. The factors evaluated on most ballots—including the one that follows—are:

Analysis	Were terms well defined?
	Was the focus on major issues?
Reasoning	Were ideas tied together in a logical way?
	Were errors in reasoning and fallacious reasoning avoided?
Evidence	Was sufficient evidence used?
	Did the evidence used meet the tests of good evidence?

Organization Were the speaker's ideas ordered clearly—in a way that was easy to follow?
If the debate was a team debate, was the overall organization of the case and sharing of responsibilities by speakers done in a well-organized manner?

Refutation Did the speaker refute the main objections expressed by the opposition?
Were the speaker's ideas reinforced during his or her rebuttal period?

Delivery Did delivery help focus attention on key ideas?
Was the speaker courteous to the opposition?

SUMMING UP

The affirmative side has the responsibility of gaining acceptance of a particular plan. The presentation of the affirmative plan, or case, is usually based on one of two strategies—a needs case or a comparative advantages case.

The negative side has the burden of clashing with the specific affirmative plan being proposed. This clash grows out of one of four main negative strategies: (1) *a defense of the* status quo, (2) *total refutation,* (3) *a minor repairs case, or* (4) *a counterplan.*

Debate takes place in a variety of settings—the classroom, at tournaments, in the courtroom—and in a variety of formats, including: the traditional, two-person, cross-examination, and a feedback format. Particular rules concerning the order of speaking and time limits are established so speakers can concentrate on major issues under the most equitable—"fairest"—conditions possible.

If you are debating in a two-person debate, you have all the responsibility to build your side's arguments while refuting your opponent's. If you are debating in a team format, those responsibilities are shared according to certain conventional guidelines and the nature of your particular case.

A debate decision is based on which side does the better job of debating. Such a decision is usually recorded on a ballot which also reflects the particular strengths and weaknesses of each speaker.

Activities

☐ Hold classroom debates on the topics you chose and phrased when you read Chapter 6.

☐ If you have time for two rounds of debate, use the traditional format for the first round and the cross-examination format for the second round. Have all debaters switch sides for the second round so everyone will gain experience presenting both affirmative and negative views.

☐ The entire class, or a selected panel of three judges, should evaluate each debate on an appropriate ballot, like the one provided in this chapter. A different person should keep time during each debate, and that person should be excused from filling out a ballot.

American Forensic Association Debate Ballot

FORM **C**

Division_____ Round_____ Room_____ Date_____ Judge_____

Affirmative_____ Negative_____

Check the column on each item which, on the following scale, best describes your evaluation of the speaker's effectiveness:

   1—poor   2—fair   3—average   4—excellent   5—superior

1st Affirmative	2nd Affirmative		1st Negative	2nd Negative
1 2 3 4 5	1 2 3 4 5		1 2 3 4 5	1 2 3 4 5
		Analysis		
		Reasoning		
		Evidence		
		Organization		
		Refutation		
		Delivery		

Total_____   Total_____   Total_____   Total_____

Team Ratings: AFFIRMATIVE: poor   fair   average   excellent   superior
               NEGATIVE: poor   fair   average   excellent   superior

Rank each debater in order of excellence (1st for best, 2nd for next best, etc.).

COMMENTS: COMMENTS:
1st Aff. (name)_____ Rank ( )   1st Neg. (name)_____ Rank ( )

2nd Aff. (name)_____ Rank ( )   2nd Neg. (name)_____ Rank ( )

In my opinion, the better debating was done by the _____
                                                    (AFFIRMATIVE OR NEGATIVE)

_____   _____
        JUDGE'S SIGNATURE   SCHOOL

Section 3

We're In This Thing Together

10

How groups work

Many students often find themselves "broke"—broke may mean anything from having to take your own popcorn to the movies to having to skip the movies altogether and babysit with your kid brother so you can afford the movies next week. If you're one of those who are often broke, you will probably try to find a good job after school hours or during the summer. Hunting a job can sometimes be a difficult business, but there are ways of making it easier.

You can get together with friends who are also hunting jobs and share information and ideas. Discussing your common goal—getting a job—can give you answers to crucial questions. (What job openings exist that you could fill? Whom do you apply to? What should you know about the employer? How much money will you get?) Sharing ideas in such an informal group discussion can be a help to everyone who participates. Job hunting—or any other difficult task—can be made easier because of the added information and the feeling of support that you can gain from discussion.

PURPOSES AND CHARACTERISTICS

A group discussion involves a small enough number of people so that everyone feels free to exchange ideas. A group discussion is also characterized by the fact that the people in the group share certain interests, problems, or goals.

In group discussion each individual shares ideas and information with others without necessarily starting from a particular point of view. The emphasis is upon cooperation—in promoting social interaction, seeking ideas, or seeking solutions. This may be contrasted with debate in which each side advocates or defends a particular position. The goal in discussion is not for any side to "win," but for the group itself to reach the best possible decision for everyone through interaction of group members.

Most discussions can be said to have one of three purposes: (1) promoting social interaction or pleasure, (2) sharing information, or (3) seeking solutions to problems confronting the group.

GROUP DISCUSSIONS FOR PLEASURE

In a discussion for pleasure, there is no particular conclusion to reach; you may simply enjoy interacting with others in the group. No doubt you belong to a group that meets together mainly because you enjoy one another's company. You meet around someone's locker every morning before school, at a certain table for lunch, or at someone's home on Saturday to listen to records and talk. When you meet, you often talk about things you're interested in just for the fun of it. Even though these meetings are very informal, they're a kind of group discussion. Family conversations can also fall into this category—as can interaction in groups that meet more formally in churches and clubs to talk about matters of common interest.

Group Discussions for Information

People often band together to increase their understanding of some area of knowledge—a church group may meet to discuss great books, for example. You may get together with three or four people to study for exams in history or science or some other subject. In that situation, you probably take turns sharing information and asking questions. You may all gain new understanding as each member of your study group explains information from his or her perspective.

Group Discussions to Solve Problems

Families frequently make decisions in order to solve problems: "There are three drivers in this family and one car. How can we most fairly and efficiently use the family car?" Similarly, people involved in school organizations, business, and government also solve problems through discussion. This kind of group discussion usually takes place in committee meetings.

As a student you may be on a committee to plan student government projects, promote more relevant courses, or improve social activities at your school. Your teachers are probably on committees too—and your parents, neighbors, and many other people you know. Most organizations and communities are run in part by committees. It's also in committees and sub-committees that legislation is hammered into form. As veteran Washington correspondent Stewart Alsop observed, "The committee system *is* the Congressional system. The fact is ... that the real work of Congress is hardly ever done on the floor of either house. It is done in committee. In committee is where reputations are made and unmade."*

There are so many committees in our society that most people serve on at least one during their lifetime. That—plus the fact that nearly everyone "discusses" something formally or informally every day—is a good reason for learning something about discussion techniques.

But first let's look at some of the reasons why discussion is such a basic part of most people's lives. What are the values of group discussion? Why do people form so many committees and other discussion groups? Let's consider too what flaws there may be in the group process.

* Stewart Alsop, *The Center: People and Power in Political Washington.* Published by Harper & Row, Publishers, Inc. Used by permission.

Values of Group Discussion

Almost everyone likes to "belong." There is a special joy in being a part of a strong family unit or a member of a special club. Being a part of a group may help you develop a sense of your own worth and allow you to grow as a person. Another value of group discussion is that talking about ideas with other people often makes the ideas easier to understand and easier to remember. It's for this reason that most teachers like to have class discussions and many students like to review for tests in small groups.

Group discussions tend to produce more acceptable decisions because more people have a part in making those decisions. If times get tougher and your family has to cut its budget, you're more likely to understand and go along with the decisions if you helped make them. No one likes to be denied a voice in decisions that affect his or her life.

Group discussions also tend to produce decisions of a better quality. In group discussions the whole answer is often more than the sum of its parts—the old "two heads (or many heads) are better than one" idea. The reason for this is that as people interact, answers come into clearer focus through questioning and new information stimulates new answers.

The principle behind representative bodies like student councils and state legislatures is that each elected member represents a larger group. It wouldn't be fair to have only a few people selected at random speak for the entire school or state—nor would it be practical for the entire student body or citizenry to meet to discuss every issue. So representatives are chosen, each of whom (in theory at least) speaks for the group that he or she represents. In a sense, then, everyone in the larger group has some voice in the decision-making process.

Flaws in Group Discussion

Although there are many good things about discussion, it is of course not always practical. Discussion is, for example, very time-consuming. It's much quicker to have the quarterback call the signals than to have eleven players talk about them before each play. Discussion can also be a complete waste of time if the individuals involved fail to reach any kind of consensus (agreement). The game would be forfeited if each player held out for his favorite play.

Another flaw which sometimes appears in group discussion is that someone may not mention the best idea—or the best idea may be rejected when mentioned—because of group pressure. Suppose you're on a committee to decide how to spend some money earned by your club. If two or three people start talking about using it for some kind of party, you may hesitate to suggest buying some new equipment. Why? Perhaps because you don't want to risk being thought of as too different, or maybe because you don't think the idea has a ghost of a chance anyway. Your idea may be the best idea—it might even be accepted by the group—but no one will know about it unless you speak up. It is true that groups will sometimes reject a good idea, but you should still try to mention any idea you have so others can at least think about it.

Good ideas may also be suppressed within the group when members don't see themselves as being of equal rank—position, popularity, or "importance." Suppose you were on a committee to discuss course offerings at your school. What kind of interaction would there be if there were three seniors and two sophomores on that committee? How would you interact if the principal and three teachers were added to the committee? In such instances those who see themselves as being of lower rank generally talk less frequently and less confidently. Those with higher rank may tend to dominate. In either case the idea of *group discussion as cooperative sharing and seeking* is being eroded.

☐ Attend a meeting of your student council, city council, church board, school board, or other organization. Listen carefully (and, if you can, take notes) so that you can answer the following questions: What seemed to be the purpose(s) of the meeting? In terms of what happened at the meeting, was the discussion valuable? Why, or why not? Was a decision actually made? Could one have been arrived at more fairly or quickly in another way?

☐ Report orally to the class about the meeting you attended. Was the discussion process successful or not as a decision-making tool? Explain your answer. If you think the meeting could have been improved, explain how.

Rank in Group Discussion According to Position, Popularity, or "Importance"

DISCUSSION FORMATS

We've classified discussion groups according to purpose: (1) pleasure, (2) information, and (3) problem-solving. They may also be classified according to the *focus* of the group. The focus of a discussion group can be *internal:* members are concerned only with interacting with one another, not with or for an audience. Another group may have an *external* focus: they would hold their discussion in front of an audience and direct what they say to that audience rather than to each other. Finally, a discussion group's focus may be *diffused:* they would actively discuss ideas *with* audience members with little or no distinction between observers and participants.

Five of the most common discussion formats are (1) the committee, (2) the panel, (3) the symposium, (4) the forum, and (5) the buzz session. These formats vary from each other in focus, and usually in purpose.

Committee

A *committee* is usually made up of individuals who share common concerns. An audience is seldom present at their meetings, so the focus of the group is internal. The committee generally has defined goals—to plan a dance, to find ways to increase business, to improve a bill. Committee goals then usually revolve around finding a solution to some problem. The committee usually has a chairperson, appointed or elected, whose job it is to keep the discussion moving and see to it that the committee does its job. (One exception to this may well be in the small group discussions you've held so far while doing the activities in this book. Your format for these has been closer to the committee format than anything else—but you have probably not chosen a chairperson.)

Some committees exist only until their assigned task is completed—until the Junior-Senior Prom is over, the Awards Ceremonies are completed, or the Watergate hearings are history. Others, called standing committees, are ongoing and continue to exist despite occasional changes in committee membership—the House Ways and Means Committee and the Senate Foreign Relations Committee, for example.

Panel

A *panel* is a group of from three to seven informed individuals who discuss a topic in front of an audience. This format is popular with classes studying discussion. The focus is both internal and external. Panel members talk among themselves (internal focus) but always loud enough so the audience can hear (external focus).

Panel members usually hold private strategy meetings before they make their presentation in front of an audience. Though each panelist is expected to have researched the topic carefully, there are to be *no formal speeches*. Panel members should be seated so that they can see one another easily and can talk to one another informally. Panels have a chairperson who has the primary responsibility of keeping the group on target so that they can suggest some solution(s) within the time alloted for their discussion. It is hoped that the group will reach consensus, but while members shouldn't choose up sides neither should they agree just for the sake of agreeing.

Panels are frequently used at PTA meetings, professional conventions, and in classrooms. The popularity of the panel format—both in and out of the classroom—may be attributed to its dual purpose and focus. Informed panelists give added information to an audience while working among themselves to solve a problem. Panelists, though acknowledging the audience's presence by the way they sit and speak, also give an audience a sense of "being in on something" as the audience watches panelists interact.

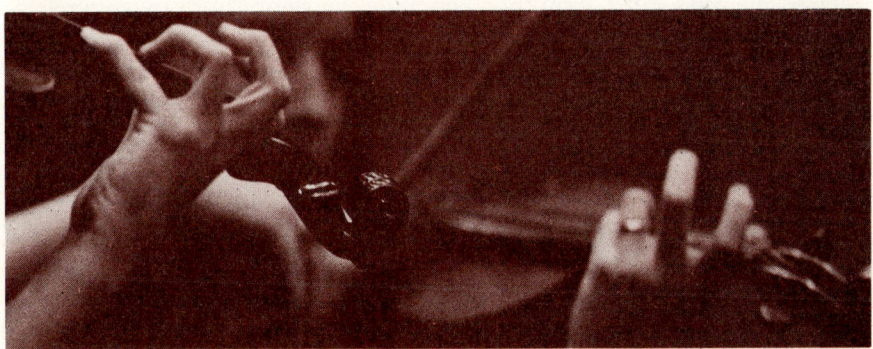

A recent panel discussion was on the topic "How can we improve our school's music program?" Panelists talked with the directors of vocal music and instrumental music. They interviewed the principal and two counselors to discuss problems about rooms and scheduling. Some of them talked with school board members while others visited other schools to find out about their music programs. Finally they worked out their agenda and discussed the problem in front of the class. Class members gained much new information from listening to the discussion, and the panelists came up with two ideas that were eventually used to improve the music program.

Symposium

A *symposium* is more formal than a panel. The focus of the symposium is external—each participant delivers a formal speech to the audience instead of discussing ideas with other participants. The purpose of the symposium is to inform audience members by exposing them to the various viewpoints of participants.

The people chosen to participate in a symposium are usually experts. Each expert is capable of speaking about the subject from the vantage point of a particular specialty. A chairperson, or moderator, usually introduces the topic and the experts. Then each expert in turn gives his or her prepared speech. For instance, a symposium dealing with the workings of your state government might feature an introduction by your history teacher, a speech on the executive branch by your governor, a speech on the legislative branch by the speaker of the house, and a speech on the judicial branch by a justice of the state supreme court. Your history teacher, the moderator, may then conclude the symposium by summarizing the various views presented. The summary might be followed by an invitation to the audience to join in a forum.

Forum

A *forum* occurs when audience members interact and question a speaker, panel members, or symposium experts. The focus is diffused since audience members and those presenting the topic interact equally. Such enlarged participation can increase everyone's knowledge and serve an advisory purpose by making the opinion of the larger group known to the "experts."

Since a forum is any situation in which audience members are free to ask questions or discuss the topic it may be combined with a lecture, panel, or symposium. Thus you may hear a meeting described as a lecture-forum, panel-forum, or symposium-forum. Or a governing body may hold a public forum—without any presentation beforehand—to discover public opinions on an issue such as a city's plan for renewing or restoring its downtown area.

In any of these instances, the chairperson is responsible for explaining the specific procedure to be followed by participants and audience members. Questions or opinions are usually directed to the chairperson, who may in turn direct them to someone else. The chairperson also keeps the forum under control and has the final responsibility of concluding the meeting—usually with a summary.

Buzz Session

This is another expanded discussion format in which audience members participate, usually after another type of presentation. The purpose of a buzz session is to involve as many people as possible in finding a solution to some problem. First, of course, everyone must be given background information. Then after a brief speech by a chairperson, or a short panel discussion or forum, the audience (or class) divides into small groups of five or six people each. These groups meet separately to discuss—hold "buzz sessions" on—the ideas already presented. In only a few minutes—under ten—each of the groups decides on a solution to the problem posed in the larger session. Then the entire audience reassembles and a representative from each small group reports—again briefly—on his or her group's proposed solution. After a summary by the chairperson, the whole group discusses the proposed solutions, and tries to decide on one.

As you can see, this format is useful with very large groups. The small group discussions use internal focus, and the representatives who report their ideas to the audience use external focus.

☐ Copy the following chart on a sheet of paper and then complete it.

FORMAT	FOCUS	PURPOSE
Committee		
Panel		
Symposium		
Forum		
Buzz Session		

☐   The class should be divided into small groups. Each group should decide what discussion format would be best for the following subjects.
   The "whys and hows" of voting in the next election
   Fighting pollution
   Choosing a vocational school or a college
   Planning a class dance

☐   What factors about the topic made your group choose a particular format? Its probable purpose? Potential audience? Size of that potential audience? Other reasons? Have someone from each group report the group's decision—and *reason for it*—to the class.

TOPICS FOR CLASSROOM DISCUSSION

Now that you know something about discussion purposes and formats, you should be ready to start working on your own discussion. The first step is finding a good topic. As with debate topics, whatever you choose should be current, controversial, and complex. Unlike debate topics, discussion topics are phrased as questions.

If you were debating the subject of fighting pollution, the debate proposition might be worded:

> Resolved: That the federal government should establish, finance, and administer programs to control air and water pollution in the United States.

If you were discussing the same general subject, the discussion question might be worded:
   How can we best combat pollution?

Such an open question encourages participants to look into the issues for possible solutions rather than to choose up sides immediately.

This also means you should avoid phrasing discussion questions in such a way that they can be answered with a simple yes or no. If you ask "Should students and faculty be prohibited from driving cars to school" you're really setting up a debate rather than a discussion, since most people will be either for or against the idea. If you're interested in discussing the problem and exploring possible solutions, you could phrase the discussion question as follows: "How can we best relieve school parking problems?"

A good topic should be worth the time you'll spend in research and in the actual classroom discussion. You caught hints of that earlier, right? Research! Obviously it's pretty hard to talk about something you don't know anything about—you can't just depend on your personal opinions to get you through. Neither should you count on the others to do all the talking—that's not fair to them or you.

You should research discussion topics as carefully as debate or speech topics so that you'll have expert opinions, statistics, and other important information at your fingertips during the discussion itself. This means taking careful notes for possible use during the discussion. It does not mean you should speak from notes or be bound by them during the discussion—unless, of course, you're part of a symposium. The emphasis in most group discussions is on interaction; you shouldn't be so glued to your notes that you don't listen to others and interact. You may occasionally want to read complex information from notes—the current Gross National Product and the percentage of the GNP based on agricultural industries—but lengthy quotes from notes tend to discourage group interaction.

GROUP PREPARATION

Two discussion formats, the panel and the symposium, require a certain amount of group preparation in addition to the individual research by participants. Such advance preparation can help the group deal with problems more effectively when presenting the actual discussion in front of the audience (or class).

If you're going to hold a panel discussion, your planning sessions should concentrate on sharing sources of information and planning the agenda (the list, in order, of the items to be discussed). Don't overdo this though; don't make the mistake of actually holding your panel discussion before you hold your panel discussion. If you start planning who will say what and when, you'll lose spontaneity and sound to your audience as if you were reading from a script.

If you're going to hold a symposium, your planning sessions will have to make clear who is going to cover what, and in what order. For instance, suppose the topic of your symposium were "How can students improve their classroom performances?" In your planning session you could divide the general topic into specific subject areas so that Steve would talk about improving in science, Christy about math, Jeff about English, Laura about history, and you would serve as the moderator to introduce the topic and summarize the thoughts of the others at the conclusion of the symposium. The order of speaking could then be determined, and individuals could begin preparing for their formal presentations.

SUMMING UP

People often form small groups to discuss common feelings or thoughts. Such group discussions may occur for pleasure, information, or to solve a particular problem.

Group discussions increase our sense of belonging and often make ideas easier to understand and remember. Decisions reached through the process of group discussion are usually also more acceptable to group members.

The discussion process is not without flaws. It is time-consuming and the best solution may sometimes be lost because of certain group pressures or perceived differences in rank by group members.

There are five basic discussion formats. These formats differ in purpose, focus, and certain procedural matters. The five discussion formats are (1) committee, (2) panel, (3) symposium, (4) forum, and (5) buzz session.

Classroom discussions may follow any of the five formats, though the panel is probably the most popular. Topics should be of current interest, controversial, and complex. Since group discussions stress cooperation rather than defending a side, discussion topics are worded as questions that encourage the presentation of various viewpoints. The presentation of these viewpoints requires as much individual research as a speech or debate, and some formats require the group to have advance planning sessions.

Activities

☐ Prepare, in writing, three discussion questions that could be used for a problem-solving discussion. Read the proposed topics to the class—having someone copy each topic on the board—and discuss the topics (current? controversial? complex? phrased to encourage various viewpoints?).

☐ As a class activity, select five topics out of all of those submitted by students in the activity above. Divide into five groups and begin preparations for discussion of the topics. Begin researching the topics now, but plan to make your presentations after you've read the next two chapters on discussion.

☐ Working with your group, decide which format would be best for the topics. If several formats seem possible, discuss them thoroughly to see if you can decide on one format that is acceptable to everyone in the group.

There Are No Small Parts, Only Small Actors

11

How to take part in a discussion

Think of the last good television show or movie that you saw. Do you remember the names of the leading actor and actress? How many of the other performers can you name? If you're like most people, you probably can't recall more than the two or three who got star billing.

Yet if that scowling actor who only appeared in one five-minute scene hadn't seemed so menacing, you wouldn't have feared for the detective's safety. If the elderly actress who appeared briefly hadn't been so convincingly snobbish, you wouldn't have laughed so hard when she got her "come-uppance." Every role is important to the overall success of the production.

The overall success of a discussion group also depends upon the individual success of each participant. But unlike an actor, a discussion participant has the choice of "playing" several roles during the course of a single discussion. No one role is assigned to anyone, but some participants fill some roles better than others and soon the other participants begin to count on them. The roles you fill may vary from group to group. Your roles change because of the different expectations of the groups, your own view of where you "fit" in each group, and how your abilities can best be used for the job at hand. The important thing to remember is to fill whatever roles you choose both well and at the appropriate times.

Important positive roles filled by discussion participants may include the following:

The Questioner   Asks for information and opinions from others.
The Contributor   Gives information and opinions about the issues being discussed.
The Reinforcer   Gives positive support to other participants by expressing agreement with their positions.
The Evaluator   Carefully analyzes each major proposal for its strengths and weaknesses.
The Compromiser   Stresses teamwork and group goals while de-emphasizing any conflicts that arise.
The Conductor   Keeps the discussion moving forward on the right track. Points out where the group has been, is, and should go.
The Summarizer   Listens well, keeps good notes, and synthesizes the work of the group at the conclusion of the discussion.

The following dialogue from the early stages of a group discussion on the topic "How can we improve the use of the school library" may serve to illustrate some of these positive roles.

KAREN: (Conductor)   Okay. Claudette has told us that most of the students she knows don't use our library to get information for reports and stuff. Al agreed with her, and probably all of us do. I think what we've got to do now is analyze the problem—Why don't more people use the library?
AL: (Contributor)   I got permission to conduct a survey in my home room and 75% of the kids said there just weren't enough new books in there that are really helpful.
CLAUDETTE: (Questioner)   What reasons did the others give for not using it?
AL: (Contributor)   Well, some said there wasn't enough room to spread things out if you were writing a report. Some others said it was too noisy to concentrate.

EVERETT: (Evaluator)   That seems a little contradictory to me, Al. On the one hand, we're saying there's a problem because not enough of us are using the library and on the other hand some students are saying it's too noisy.

CYNTHIA: (Compromiser)   Everett, it seems to me that it doesn't take more than two or three people to make lots of noise. Two or three could make enough noise so that none of us could study even if we were scattered around the library so I don't think there's any conflict between what some of the kids in Al's room said and what we see as a problem.

HARRY: (Reinforcer)   I think Cynthia's right—and Al too. I didn't conduct a survey in my homeroom, but I did ask a dozen of my friends about the library. Only two of them said they ever use it. The others gave the same reasons for not using it that Al found.

KAREN: (Conductor)   Okay, we've got three reasons for not using the library—not enough good new books, not enough room, and it's too noisy. Unless anyone else has some other reasons for not using the library, what we ought to look at next are the reasons we don't have enough good books or space. Before we do that though, does anyone else have another reason for the library's not being used much?

SMALL ACTORS

You can see that there aren't any "small parts" in discussions—everyone can take an important part if he or she wants to contribute. However, there is sometimes a "small actor" or two—a participant who, like the occasional temperamental performer in show business, has to have his or her way—or sometimes holds things back. People don't usually mean to act like small actors, and often don't even know that they're doing it, but the results of such "smallness" still hurt the group. It is more often "small actors" than it is lack of research that cause discussions to break down.

Here are some small actor "roles" to avoid:

Small Actor Role #1: Ever Emotional becomes so involved in the discussion that he or she makes rash statements and over-reacts to others' statements. For example, if someone in the group said "Senator Smith would make a great President," Ever might shout "Oh yeah? That's the dumbest thing I've ever heard of!" Could be—but saying so won't move the discussion forward. Ever would probably be better off keeping personal feelings out of it for the moment and asking a factual question, like "What bills did Senator Smith vote for last session?" If it turns out Smith didn't even show up for most votes, or voted for bills most people in the group are against, it probably won't be long before all the other participants agree with Ever—and what's more, they'll know why.

Small Actor Role #2: Always Anxious is overly concerned with adhering to the agenda. Anxious wants to move quickly down the list of things to be discussed so the meeting can be adjourned early. Anxious can't understand why some people want to keep talking. After all, it's more important to follow the proper pattern—and get through in record time—than it is to come up with a real solution. Isn't it?

Small Actor Role #3: Forever Friendly smiles and speaks in conversational tones. Friendly *knows* what roles to play at what times—when to give a supportive nod, when to ask a question for clarification, when to add information or sum up what's been said. Friendly's real concern is making a good impression. Friendly only asks questions that can't possibly make him or her look ignorant. This attitude is rather strange when you consider the fact that our astronauts—an intelligent and highly skilled group—constantly ask questions and check out information during preparation periods and their actual missions.

Small Actor Role #4: Completely Closed sees no reason to be open-minded since he or she already has all the right answers. Completely Closed won't risk seeming "weak" by changing his or her mind even if there's a good reason to—and there often is, either before or during a discussion.

For example, not long ago a classroom group set out to discuss the question, "How can we best find and remove all the chiselers from the welfare roles?" At first, everyone in the group shared the bias expressed in the question. However, since they weren't sure of a solution and since they needed more information, they set to work researching the topic with open minds. After much leg-work and dozens of interviews, they found that most people on welfare are not "chiselers." The group then came to class and discussed a new question: "How can we improve the welfare system?" Unlike Completely Closed, they hadn't been afraid to change their minds when they learned more about the topic.

Small Actor Role #5: Jolly Joker figures the discussion isn't very important anyway, so why not use the time to display his or her wit. (Or lack of it.) Jolly Joker uses other people's remarks as "straight" lines to which he or she can add a punch line. If the rest of the group actually finds such remarks funny, the occasional bits of humor may be a help in providing temporary relaxation. However, when Jolly becomes offensive, boring, or excessive in the desire to entertain, the group is likely to accomplish less and less.

As with the positive roles discussed earlier, those filling negative roles do so because of the different expectations of the group, their own views of their abilities and how they "fit" into a group. You can reduce others' tendencies to take on "small actor roles" *by not* locking them into the role ("you get so emotional all the time") and *by* encouraging them to take on a more positive role.

Whatever positive roles you assume in a group, you must be prepared in advance through research and prepared during the discussion to listen.

A good group discussion demands good listening because the discussion process is one of building and refining ideas through interaction. Yet, all too often people miss what is being said because they're planning how they're going to "slip in a good one"—some rare bit of information that will make them look good or some strong bit of refutation of an idea. As we suggested earlier, hear people and ideas out before judging them. If you're not sure what was meant by a statement, ask for clarification or repeat what you think was said to make sure you've got it. Such careful listening helps maintain the needed spirit of cooperation and keeps the discussion group moving toward its goal.

☐ Have the class choose a topic of discussion that you could talk on without extensive research:
    problems related to the school lunch hour
    the problem of choosing three new courses to be taught at your school
    _____ (your choice)

☐ After the topic has been chosen, divide into groups of 6 or 7 members apiece. Your teacher can then distribute slips of paper to each of you designating a particular role (positive or negative) to be played during a ten-minute discussion. Roles should be relatively evenly divided between positive and negative in each of the groups.

☐ Do not tell anyone what role you get—reveal it only through your actions and remarks during the discussion.

☐ After ten minutes of the problem-solving discussion, stop and write down what roles you think the others in your group were playing. After everyone has written down his or her guesses compare them with the actual roles the teacher assigned.

☐ Were some roles easier to spot than others? Why? In what ways did the different roles help or hinder your group in arriving at a solution?

The Process of Group Discussion

Just as a good scenario, or outline, is a key to the success of a film, so a plan of action is important in a discussion. A discussion "scenario" usually progresses through a series of steps leading up to a final goal. In problem-solving discussions, the pattern most frequently suggested contains six basic steps.

1. *Introduction of the Topic*

   Define the topic; what is the problem?

   Why does the group consider it a problem?

   Why must it be dealt with?

   What limitations should be placed on the discussion of the topic —should your group talk only about certain aspects of the problem since other aspects of it are out of your control?

2. *Analysis of the Problem*

   An investigation of the problem and presentation of information to answer such questions as:

   What are the causes of the problem?

   How long has it been a problem?

   How have people tried to handle the problem?

   Have any measures helped—at least in part?

3. *Establish the Standards for the Solution*

   What goals does the group hope to accomplish by the solution? Is there an order of importance—a set of priorities—for those goals?

   (For instance, a committee may have to decide whether it's more important to cut costs or improve education.)

4. *Brainstorming Possible Solutions*

   What ideas can you offer that might possibly serve as a solution? (NOTE: In the brainstorming stage of a discussion, members of the group should be free to toss out any ideas they want. The purpose here is to suggest as many possibilities—no matter how improbable they seem—as you can. This portion of the discussion should be free-wheeling and uncritical—with no one playing the evaluator role—so the group will have as many solutions to consider as possible.)

5. *Testing of Solutions*

   Apply the criteria, or standards, set up in step 3 to each solution suggested in step 4.

   Is there one particular solution that seems to meet most criteria, and gives promise of successfully solving the problem?

   Should a particular proposal be amended or two or three proposals combined to solve the problem?

   Can the group reach general agreement on the solution to the problem?

   If not, you may go back to step 4—or maybe even to step 2.

   If you can agree on a solution, then you are ready for step 6.

6. *Taking Action*

   Hours of research and discussion shouldn't be wasted. If your group is successful enough to arrive at a mutually agreed upon solution, you should push on to see that the solution is carried out.

Your group may not follow this problem-solving pattern rigidly. Groups quite often jump from one point to another. You may discover in evaluating a proposed solution (step 5) that you haven't talked about what now seems an important criterion (step 3). Still, it's a good idea to start with a logical pattern in mind—it should make for a more productive discussion. While the chairperson has the primary responsibility for helping the discussion progress in an orderly pattern, all participants should be aware of the pattern and do their best to follow it.

The Importance of a Good Set

Actors need stage sets designed to allow them freedom of movement. Similarly, a discussion "set" should encourage freedom of interaction.

☐ Which of the following seating patterns do you think would encourage the most interaction among group members and with the chairperson (heavy dot)? Which would discourage interaction? In which might the chairperson tend to dominate the group? Participate as part of the group?

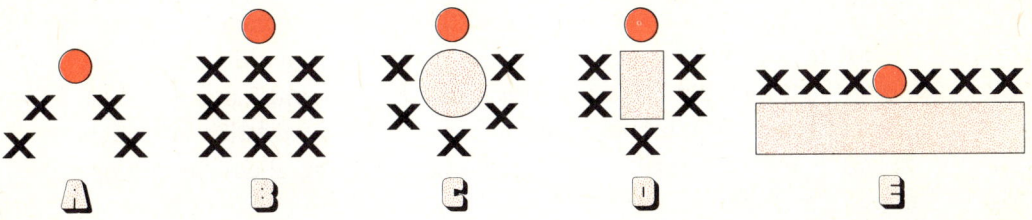

The interaction that takes place in a group depends upon spatial relationships—seating arrangements. You tend to talk to those people you can see easily. It's most difficult to maintain eye contact with people who are seated at your side (E) and those obstructed by other people (B). (E) might be a good arrangement for a symposium, but not for a committee meeting. (B) might work when reporting back from a buzz session—but for the small group discussion part, (C) would probably be best.

Another factor which influences interaction is the size of the group. Larger groups (B) seldom have the interaction of smaller groups (A)—again, because you tend to talk to those people you can look at easily. Large groups tend to inhibit interaction or divide again into subgroups, and small groups often fail to provide the variety of opinions needed to arrive at the best solution to a problem. Because group interaction and varied opinions are so important to the success of the discussion process, the ideal number of participants is five to seven.

Evaluating Your Discussion Group

The real credit for the success (or lack of it) of a group discussion belongs to the group as a whole. In evaluating the discussion, group members and observers (if any) should first ask "Did the group accomplish what it set out to do?"

If the group was attempting to solve a problem, did they:
Analyze the problem in depth?
Establish criteria by which to judge suggested solutions?
Consider and test several solutions?
Agree to take action on a particular solution?

If the group was sharing information with an audience, did they:
Cover the topic thoroughly and from various points of view?
Receive positive audience response?

Though ideally you should evaluate the group as a whole, it can also be useful to evaluate or record what individuals did within the group. Seldom do all members interact or contribute in an equal manner. The number of times an individual talks is hardly a good yardstick by which to judge his or her contributions since it says nothing about the quality of those remarks.

The following guidelines may be used to evaluate the interaction and contributions of individual participants.

Attitude	Did the participant show a spirit of cooperation? Help search for a group solution? Acknowledge and reinforce ideas of others?
Knowledge	Did the participant contribute needed information to the group? Contribute criteria and/or possible solutions?
Analysis	Did the participant evaluate ideas? Ask questions when they were needed for clarification?
Relevancy	Did the participant listen well to others? Contribute ideas that built on to what had already been said? Contribute at "the right time" in terms of the overall outline or pattern of the discussion? Help keep the discussion moving?

SUMMING UP

A successful discussion will probably be one in which five to seven participants (1) play various positive roles at appropriate times, (2) recognize the worth of the others in the group and contribute and react without undue emotion or haste, (3) attempt to follow a logical process of development, and (4) arrange themselves in a seating pattern suitable for good interaction.

Activities

☐ Attend a group meeting (government, school, church, or club). If possible, attend the meeting with three or four other students. Write up an individual report to be presented orally to the class. If others attended the same meeting, a comparison of reports can be made by the class. Report on:
    a. the roles played by various members of the group
    b. the effects of seating arrangements on interaction
    c. the process—or steps—followed by the group as it attempted to accomplish its goals
    d. any problem that prevented the group from accomplishing its goals

☐ If any of your local television stations broadcast panels or forums, watch one and report on it. Base your report on the same items listed above. Also indicate whether or not the presence of television lights and cameras seemed to have any effect on the participants or on the overall discussion.

☐ The next time you attend a meeting of a group that you belong to, (a) try playing a different positive role in the group and (b) sit in a different chair. Were there any changes in the way(s) people communicated with you? Discuss any changes with others in the class.

WHO'S IN CHARGE AROUND HERE? 12

How to chair a discussion group

When things are going smoothly, you hardly notice the hard work of the people around you. Ah, but when things go wrong! If it's time for the dance to begin but there's no band, it's "Who's in charge of getting the entertainment?" If your favorite piece of legislation doesn't get out of committee in time to be considered this session, it's "Who's in charge of that committee?"

How Who's In Charge Gets That Way

People in charge of formal groups, like program committees and congressional committees, are usually elected or appointed to their positions of leadership. Informal groups often operate without any designated leader—and yet, as you've probably noticed, one or two people eventually lead the group in arriving at many of its decisions. Such leaders are said to *emerge* from the group.

Why do certain people become leaders and not others? Think of the leaders you know—of both formal and informal groups—and try to answer that question. You may find that many of them have emerged as leaders because they seem to have taken the following points as a list of personal rules. If you're interested in being the one in charge yourself, A, B, C, and D may put you on the road to leadership.

Always talk up when you have something concrete to say. Others need to know that you're really interested in the group and its goals. Constant meaningless chatter doesn't impress anyone—but silence can be taken as disinterest. Your remarks don't always have to be contributions of information. Remember the other positive roles. You can lead by making procedural statements or asking good questions of other discussion participants. The ability to speak up and bring about an effective compromise between conflicting viewpoints is even more certain to stamp you as having leadership potential.

Be responsible. Sometimes people want the rewards of leadership without the responsibilites. Attend group sessions regularly and be willing to work at any assignment, no matter how small it seems, that advances the group's goals.

Compliment others when they deserve it. People like others who make them feel important and who recognize their accomplishments. If someone shares a fine idea or does well on a project, let that person know you appreciate it. Don't, however, compliment people when you don't feel they deserve it—to do so makes you lose some of your credibility.

Demonstrate knowledge. If you don't know what's going on, no amount of talking will turn you into a leader. The leader of the band had better know more about music in general than the person playing first trumpet. The speaker of the house should know the rules of the house at least as well as any other representative. Acquiring knowledge requires effort—reading, listening, practice, etc.—but then, so does being a leader.

☐ Divide into small groups. Each group should list three people whom it considers effective leaders, in national politics, school or community affairs, for example. What characteristics have helped them emerge as good leaders?

☐ What, if anything, should be added to the A, B, C, D list? How do these ways to leadership differ from our suggestions for being a good participant?

☐ Compare your conclusions with those of other groups.

Types of Leadership

"Who's in charge around here?" There could be several different answers to that question. From one group someone may speak up and say "You'd better believe I am!" A second group of people look at one another, shrug shoulders, raise their eyebrows, speak all at once for a minute, and then lapse into silence. In a third group, Louise says that she starts the discussions, Mark promotes group harmony and interaction, Larry keeps the group on course, and Barbara is usually the one who prompts the group to take some action.

These three responses represent the three types of group leadership. (1) *Authoritarian* One person is very much in command. (2) *Laissez-faire* Laissez-faire essentially means "let the people do what they want." A chairperson with this philosophy gives no direction and the group becomes virtually leaderless. (3) *Democratic leadership* Most people in the group feel free to lead the discussion at some particular point. Responsibilities are shared according to the particular talents and drives of those in the group.

There are no doubt many factors that influence the kind of leadership present in a discussion group. The main ones, though, are (1) the personalities of group members and of the chairperson, (2) the purposes of the group, (3) the size of the group, and (4) the time allotted for discussion.

Authoritarian leadership is most likely to occur when one strong personality is present in the group. That person often emerges as a leader even if he or she isn't officially chairperson. The authoritarian leader decides what ideas will be discussed, how much time will be spent talking about each idea, which members will get to talk about them, and often forces the group to accept his or her opinion as the answer to any problem. Authoritarian leadership is called for when a large group is confronted with a complex task to be accomplished in a short time. If the senior class, for example, were only given one period to decide what gift to leave the school, it would be good if they had a strong class president to lead their discussion. The president would have to discourage all lengthy or irrelevant remarks. The class would only have a minimum amount of time to set up criteria and propose solutions because they have to arrive at their decision in less than an hour.

Authoritarian leadership has the advantage of being sure of keeping the group to its appointed task. Each group member knows where he or she stands in relationship to the leader and to the decision-making process. But there are also some disadvantages to authoritarian leadership. Because of the strong hand of the leader and the speed of the process, good ideas are sometimes lost—some are never even presented. Authoritarian leadership tends to discourage some participants, even to the point of making them very reluctant group members.

A **laissez-faire** approach is most likely to occur when group members feel no strong committment to a purpose and no urgency of time. Informal, social gatherings tend to thrive with such relaxed leadership. Frequently when such groups (whether a neighborhood club or a group of retired citizens) find a sense of purpose or have a specific task to accomplish, some leadership emerges, at least until the task has been completed.

A "leader" with a *laissez-faire* attitude doesn't want to have any control over the group; so he or she prepares no agenda, lets people talk whenever they feel like it, and never reminds the group of the task at hand. Thus, *laissez-faire* groups frequently "go off" the subject. This lack of attention to organization and the task at hand frequently leads to a failure to interact and arrive at a satisfactory conclusion.

A **democratic leader** seeks to make full use of the talents of all group members. Members are encouraged to react to one another's statements. A democratic leader seeks to make clear the task at hand and the procedure to be followed in discussing the problem. At the same time, he or she encourages the sharing of varied viewpoints and the careful evaluation of all ideas—including those of the leader.

A good *democratic leader* shares leadership responsibilities with others in the group. This allows the designated leader some freedom to express ideas as a group member in addition to leading the discussion. The sharing of responsibilities also strengthens members' identification with the group and promotes a better climate for the exchange of ideas.

Though Arnie may be in charge of planning the discussion and guiding it through the agenda, Linda will feel more group spirit if she knows she is to lead off the discussion. Leslie may be asked to encourage everybody to participate during the discussion, and Bonnie—as the calm, popular one of the group—may assume the responsibility of handling any personality conflicts that arise during the discussion. By having four members share leadership responsibilities, Arnie is freed to contribute more ideas and three more people will feel an extra bit of committment to the group's goal.

☐ In the groups you belong to, which types of leadership have you seen exhibited?

☐ Which kind of leadership do you enjoy most when you are a group member?

☐ Which kind of leader do you think you are (or would be) as a chairperson?

WHAT TO DO IF YOU'RE THE ONE IN CHARGE

The person in charge of a discussion is expected to carry out certain leadership responsibilities—or share some of them as he or she sees fit.

Leadership responsibilities usually fall into the following five categories:
1. Planning the discussion
2. Initiating the discussion
3. Directing the discussion
4. Promoting interaction
5. Handling personality conflicts.

Planning the Discussion

For most formal discussions the leader or chairperson is expected to prepare the agenda for the group meeting—a list of items to be discussed, in the order in which they will be discussed. An agenda may also indicate an appropriate amount of time allotted to the discussion of each item.

In preparing an agenda, chairpeople often consult the others in the group to find out what they want to discuss. The chairperson should prepare and distribute the agenda well in advance of the discussion meeting. That way, group members will have a chance to think about the agenda in advance and they will be more likely to be well prepared for the discussion.

Initiating the Discussion

The leader has the responsibility of getting the discussion started on time. If the members of the discussion do not know one another, the leader should take time to have them introduce themselves. If there is an audience, the leader should open the discussion by introducing himself or herself and all the participants.

Then, whether there is an audience or not, the leader should get things underway by stating the subject and the purpose(s) of the discussion. If the group is meeting as a committee, the chairperson should begin by explaining the first item on the agenda. For a symposium, the moderator will state the topic, how the background of each expert relates to that topic, and then turn the program over to the first symposium speaker. For a panel discussion, a brief explanation of the discussion question should be enough to get people talking. If the group is slow to respond, the leader may ask for additional information about the problem or ask for suggestions about how to approach the first item on the agenda.

Directing the Discussion

Though it is possible to be too anxious about the agenda, most groups seem to err in the other direction. A participant wants to explain how Uncle Frank dealt with a similar problem, which reminds another participant of a funny story about Aunt Kate, and then.... It's easy for people to get off the track—but a major part of any chairperson's job is to keep them from doing just that.

If the group is going to accomplish its goals within the time allotted, the leader must see to it that the subject is dealt with in some systematic fashion. It is the leader who is responsible for setting up and sticking to a "scenario," as described in Chapter 11, pp. 155-56. Occasional anecdotes and bits of humor help relieve tensions and strengthen group spirit —but even allowing for that, the leader must keep bringing the group back to the topic.

A leader must point out relationships between key ideas, make needed transitions, and provide "internal summaries" as well as a summary of various viewpoints at the conclusion of the discussion. An example of a leader's "moving the group" follows. In this example, the leader provides an internal summary—pointing out what the group has already done—and seeks to have them take the next step in their "scenario" by asking them some leading questions.

LEADER: You've all pointed out some real problems with public transportation in our city—it doesn't reach many parts of town, it's slow, the equipment is old and often breaks down, and ridership is declining—threatening to close down the system or force prices above what many people can pay. We could probably continue to give more examples to illustrate these problems, but—with only thirty minutes left, I think it's time we tried to establish our priorities. Which of these problems is the most serious? Which must our solution deal with first? Okay, Carolyn, do you want to say something first?

Promoting Interaction

Ideally, everyone in a discussion group should have equal opportunities to present information and suggestions; that's what discussion is all about. The conclusion(s), again ideally, should reflect the knowledge and views of the entire group as much as possible. But, realistically, individual differences are going to make people's contributions vary. Some people tend to talk a lot and push hard for acceptance of their ideas while others are quiet and give in easily.

Most discussion leaders try to seek some kind of balance in the contributions of group members. Good leaders try to encourage the quiet people to speak more often, and to tone down those who always have more than enough to say. If a person hesitates to contribute, try calling on that person from time to time—but make sure you give advance warning. *Don't say,* "Harold, you haven't said anything yet. What do you think about this idea?" *Instead, say* something like, "Before we decide what to do, let's make sure we've heard everyone's ideas. I'll go over what we've said

so far and then we can go around the table and see if there are more viewpoints." This approach gives Harold some warning; he knows he's going to have to say something, but at least he has a chance to think it over first.

"Hesitant Harold" may be less of a problem to a discussion group and its leader than "Motormouth"—the group member who never stops talking. How can you effectively and tactfully control the Motormouths of this world? The problem is that telling Motormouth to be quiet may result in just that—quiet on everyone's part. Everyone may feel so intimidated that the whole discussion just stops. You may have to be more subtle than that with Motormouth. One approach might be to ask for a summary: "Could you summarize your main point for us, Motormouth? Then, I think we should hear from someone else."

Handling Personality Conflicts

People working together on important issues are bound to experience differences of opinion. After all, if everyone in the group agreed completely, there wouldn't be much need for a discussion.

For a group to function effectively, differences of opinion should focus on issues—not personalities. (Remember the first of the "Slovenly Seven"—the fallacy of an *ad hominem* argument or personal attack?) A good leader seeks to prevent personality clashes or at least tries to divert them so they don't cause a breakdown of the group process by upsetting everyone and distracting them from the subject. Occasionally it is necessary to remind members of the need for self-control; preferably, you can fend off emotional clashes by summing up opposing viewpoints in calm, objective language.

Note the way Carol attempts to fend off a possible emotional clash between Ted and Marcia.

TED: I think Marcia's idea of a school carnival is just kinda dumb—it's so old fashioned. We need to do something a lot more modern.

CAROL: Everyone seems to agree we need to raise money for the project. Marcia's suggestion was the first proposed solution—and certainly we need to consider other possible solutions—but first let's look at Marcia's idea more thoroughly. The carnival has worked at some schools, as Marcia pointed out.

On the other hand, a lot of students may want to try something else. It's possible we might have some popular music or up-date the carnival in other ways. First, let's let Marcia explain her idea in more detail.

As you can see, the responsibilities of leadership are varied and demanding. "Who's in charge around here?" Hopefully it's someone capable of handling the various responsibilities of leadership, or knowledgeable enough to have some members of the group share in those responsibilities.

EVALUATING YOUR DISCUSSION LEADER

The following guidelines will help you to determine just how well a discussion leader has met his or her responsibilities.

Did the leader plan the discussion well? Clearly explain the purpose of the discussion? Appropriately introduce members and/or the topic? Help guide the participants toward the group's goal? Promote "balanced" interaction among participants? Help the participants avoid personality conflicts—or help resolve them if any arose?

SUMMING UP

While some leaders are appointed to their positions, others emerge from the group. Those emergent leaders seem to be the ones who talk up, are responsible, compliment others, and demonstrate knowledge of the topic and of discussion procedure.

Leaders are usually classified as being authoritarian, *laissez-faire,* or democratic. The *laissez-faire* leader assumes few, if any, of the responsibilities of leadership. The authoritarian leader takes all the responsibilities as his or her own. The democratic leader shares leadership responsibilities with participants willing and skillful enough to assume them.

The leadership responsibilities common to all discussion formats stressing cooperative interaction are: (1) planning the discussion, (2) initiating the discussion, (3) directing the discussion, (4) promoting interaction, and (5) handling personality conflicts.

Activities

☐ If you attended a public meeting as suggested in the first chapter in this section, discuss the type of leadership exhibited at that meeting. Did the leader exhibit the qualities mentioned in this chapter? Did the leader seem to have the respect and cooperation of the group? How could you tell? Which of the five responsibilities of leadership did the leader carry out effectively?

☐ Have you observed anyone who can handle all five leadership responsibilities successfully? Who? What was there about that person and his or her group that helped him or her lead so successfully?

☐ Present your in-class problem-solving panel discussion.
   a. Have others evaluate your group in terms of the criteria given in Chapter 11.
   b. After the discussion, participants should indicate the roles they thought *all* group members played.
   c. Have the participants compare their evaluations with one another and with audience members.
   d. Did you sense any small actors in your group? Were you one at times?
   e. Evaluate your group leader in terms of the criteria on page 170. Have those in your class who were not part of your discussion group also evaluate the leader. Discuss and compare your evaluations, and explain how you arrived at your conclusions.

A FINAL NOTE

You communicate with others in many ways.

> as an individual entertaining, sharing ideas, or persuading other people;
> as an individual debating with another over which of two alternatives is better;
> as part of a group enjoying one another's company, providing information for others, or seeking to solve a problem.

Your understanding of the processes of public speaking, debate, and group discussion has hopefully been increased by reading this book. I hope too that your skills have been sharpened by the various activities throughout the book. Many of the basic skills (reasoning, research, adapting to others, outlining, delivery) are common to all three processes—public speaking, debate, and group discussion.

Often you go from one to the other rather quickly. You may urge the building of a new tennis court, be challenged to debate the issue, and—as a result of the debate—be in a group to discuss the problems of how and where the new courts should be built.

A legislator proposes a new bill, it's debated, and it's sent to committee. An amended bill comes out of committee, is debated anew in Congress, and is endorsed by a legislator in a public speech on the campaign trail.

You have by now given a speech, debated, and participated in a group discussion. These were separate activities, but more often than not they're inter-related.

☐ Let the class choose to "be":
   a. your state legislature
   b. the United States Senate or House of Representatives
   c. the United Nations General Assembly

☐ If you chose (a) or (b), find out current issues being debated and the positions of the political parties on those issues. Let the class divide into political parties seeking to have certain bills adopted. Research the bills carefully as you prepare to speak for or against them.

☐ Congressional bills must be reported out of committees. Study the nature of the committees in (a) or (b) and organize three or four of the major committees to consider and report out bills. Present and debate the bills "on the floor."

☐ Find out the rules that govern the procedures in the governing body you've chosen. Most parliamentary procedure is governed by *Robert's Rules of Order.* * A key to getting anything done in Congress is knowledge of the rules governing Congress.

☐ If you chose (c) have each of you represent a country in the United Nations. Research that country and its interests carefully. Introduce to your "fellow delegates" a matter that currently concerns that country and also seek to support its best interests in any debate or committee action.

---

* *Robert's Rules of Order Newly Revised,* Glenview, Illinois: Scott, Foresman and Co., 1970.

BOOKS TO READ

You can read from the following list to gain greater understanding of:

Public Speaking

Contemporary American Speeches: A Source Book of Speech, by Wil A. Linkugel, et al. Belmont, Calif.: Wadsworth Publishing Co., 1972. (Interesting collection of speeches by the famous and not so famous.)

Informative Speaking, by Thomas H. Olbricht. Glenview, Ill.: Scott, Foresman, 1968. (Excellent chapters on ways of clarifying meaning and on the language of informative speaking.)

In Pursuit of Peace: Speeches of the Sixties, Donald W. Zacharias, ed. New York: Random House, 1970. (Ten speeches of the sixties by such divergent people as Senators Goldwater and Fulbright.)

Persuasive Speaking, by Thomas M. Scheidel. Glenview, Ill.: Scott, Foresman, 1967. (Presents both classical and modern approaches to persuasion.)

Public Speaking as a Liberal Art, by John F. Wilson and Carroll G. Arnold. Boston: Allyn and Bacon, 1974. (Good chapters on discovering ideas and building proof and on style and delivery.)

Speech Communication 2nd ed., by William D. Brooks. Dubuque: Wm. C. Brown Co., 1974. (Excellent section focusing on speaker, message, and audience.)

The Art of Persuasion, 2nd ed., by Wayne C. Minnick. Boston: Houghton Mifflin, 1968. (Emphasizes the importance of audience analysis and adaptation.)

The Message The Speaker The Audience, by John Hasling. New York: McGraw-Hill, 1971. (Suggestions on organizing material, preparing and practicing your delivery.)

The Rhetoric of the Civil Rights Movement, by Haig A. Bosmajian and Hamida Bosmajian. New York: Random House, 1969. (Numerous speeches and a debate by spokesmen of the movement.)

Time to Speak, by Wil A. Linkugel and David M. Berg. Belmont, Calif.: Wadsworth Publishing Co., 1970. (Offers suggestions to help speakers be relevant, clear, interesting, and believable.)

Listening

Human Listening, by Carl H. Weaver. Indianapolis: The Bobbs-Merril Co., 1972. (Emphasizes not only "what the listener can do to improve," but "what the talker can do to help.")

Listening Behavior, by Larry L. Barker. Englewood Cliffs, N.J.: Prentice-Hall, 1971. (Analyzes the listening process and discusses some factors which may influence listening behavior.)

Debate

Argumentation and Debate, by James H. McBurney and Glen E. Mills. New York: Macmillan Co., 1964. (Emphasizes the importance of debate and the value of training in debate.)

Argumentation and Debate: Rational Decision Making, 3rd ed., by Austin J. Freeley. Belmont, Calif.: Wadsworth Publishing Co., 1971. (Includes examples of both traditional and cross-examination debate.)

Argumentation and Rational Debating, by Robert C. Dick. Dubuque: Wm. C. Brown Co., 1972. (Chapters on evidence, reasoning, cases, refutation and rebuttal, and composition and delivery.)

Modern Argumentation and Debate: Principles and Practices, by Wayne N. Thompson. New York: Harper & Row, Publishers, 1971. (Offers not only general theory, but practical advice for improving your ability to debate.)

Strategies for Educational Debate, by William C. Colburn. Boston: Holbrook Press, 1972. (Excellent chapters on analysis, case development, and the responsibilities of debaters. Included is the 1966 intercollegiate championship debate.)

Group Discussion

Discussion and Group Methods: Theory and Practice, by Ernest G. Bormann. New York: Harper & Row, Publishers, 1969. (Good chapters on group discussions and discussion leadership.)

Effective Group Discussion, by John K. Brilhart. Dubuque: Wm. C. Brown Co., 1974. (Easy-to-read paperback with good chapters on organizing discussions and observing and evaluating discussions.)

Effective Small Group Communication, by Ernest and Nancy Bormann. Minneapolis: Burgess Publishing Co., 1972. (Excellent advice for dealing with problems created by group members and those created by the group.)

The Dynamics of Discussion, by Dean C. Barnlund. Boston: Houghton Mifflin, 1960. (Delves into group discussion to study the interpersonal relationships involved.)

The Miracle of Dialogue, by Reuel L. Howe. New York: The Seabury Press, 1963. (Offers insights into improving group relationships at home, in churches, and on the job.)

Parliamentary Procedure

Meeting Management, by Henry L. Ewbank, Jr. Dubuque: Wm. C. Brown Co., 1968. (Discusses parliamentary motions as well as organizational and procedural structures and strategies.)

Modern Parliamentary Procedure, by Ray E. Keesey. Boston: Houghton Mifflin, 1974. (Sketches historical development of parliamentary procedure and also discusses rules, motions, and duties of those in charge of meetings.)

Robert's Rules of Order Newly Revised, by Henry M. Robert, et al. Glenview, Ill.: Scott, Foresman, 1970. (Generally considered *the* authority on parliamentary procedure.)

Glossary of Terms

affirmative: that side, in a debate, which supports a particular change in the *status quo*. The affirmative argues *for* the debate proposition.

agenda: the "ordering" of the items to be discussed in a group meeting.

argument: in debate, a conclusion reached after examining evidence.

authoritarian leadership: process of leadership in which one person is very much in command—deciding what ideas will be discussed, how much time will be spent talking about each idea, which members will get to talk, and often what the final decision will be.

case: the formal statement, development, and proof of your point of view.

committee: a group of people sharing common concerns with generally defined goals. An audience is seldom present at their meetings so the focus of the group is internal.

credibility: the *believability* of a speaker because the person is viewed as being honest, knowledgable, and having the best interests of the listeners at heart.

debate: formal type of argument designed to test the merits of a particular conclusion or solution.

deductive reasoning: a process beginning with a generally held truth, called a *major premise*, and arriving, often via a specific instance, called a *minor premise*, at a *conclusion* about a particular person or principle.

democratic leadership: a process by which the leader seeks to make clear the task at hand and the procedure to be followed, while encouraging group interaction and the full use of the talents of all group members.

fallacies: errors in reasoning.

feedback: verbal or nonverbal responses from listeners that tell a speaker how he or she is doing. Feedback is frequently given after a speech, but it is also an ongoing process during a speech.

forum: a discussion format in which audience members interact among themselves or with a speaker, panel members, or symposium experts.

group discussion: a process of cooperative interaction by people who feel free to exchange ideas. Group discussions may be for the purpose of promoting social interaction, sharing information, or seeking solutions to problems confronting the group.

inductive reasoning: a process beginning with *specific* facts or instances and building from them to a *general* statement or principle.

laissez-faire leadership: process of leadership in which the chairperson gives no direction and "lets the people do what they want."

negative: that side, in a debate, which opposes the debate proposition. The negative must clash directly with the arguments of the affirmative side.

nonverbal communication: meaning received or sent by such ways as movement, gestures, variations in vocal characteristics, facial expression, eye contact, seating arrangements, etc.

panel: a small group of informed people who discuss a topic in front of an audience. Panel members interact among themselves and give no formal speeches.

proposition: the subject of a debate. A carefully worded statement that indicates the particular position being supported by the affirmative.

reasoning: the process by which you attempt to establish a relationship between your supporting material and your position.

rebuttal: a speech designed to refute your opponent's arguments and rebuild your own.

refutation: the process of attacking your opponent's arguments.

statistics: information presented in numerical form to reflect particular conditions at a particular time. To be effective, they must be up-to-date, representative, and accurately recorded.

status quo: the current situation; the present way of doing things.

stock issues: questions meant to reveal the issues of any policy debate.

supportive materials: data chosen to make a speaker's purpose clear and acceptable to the audience. Five types are examples, visual aids, testimony, comparisons, and statistics.

symposium: format in which each participant delivers a formal speech to the audience instead of discussing ideas with other participants. Participants should be experts who can give listeners new viewpoints about an idea or problem.

testimony: a statement quoted by a speaker showing that someone else—usually an expert—agrees with the point the speaker is making.

Index

Adapting to audiences, on the basis of
   attitudes toward topic, 9-11
   demographic factors, 5-8, 11
   feedback, 59-60, 63-64, 124
   prior knowledge about topic, 11
   time limitations, 11
Ad Hominem attacks, 105-106, 111, 169
Affirmative side
   defined, 70, 79
   duties of, 82, 113-114
   plan, 87-89
   speaker responsibilities, 125-128
   strategies, 114-116, 125-128
Agenda, 145, 164, 166
Agnew, Spiro, 40
Alliteration, 40
Alsop, Stewart, 136
"Always Anxious", 152
Appearance, importance of, 46, 54, 56
Argument, as a special term in debate, 89, 93-94, 97, 113-114, 116-117, 120, 122-123, 125-128
Aristotle, 5-6
Authoritarian leadership, 163-164, 170

Ballot, for debate, 130
Begging the Question, 105-106, 111
Black's Law Dictionary, 82
Body language, 54-55, 62
Body movement, 47-49, 54-56
Bradbury, Ray, 77
Brainstorming, 156
Buckley, William F., 22
Burden of proof, 113, 116-118, 120, 126-127
Burden of rebuttal, 127-128
Buzz session, 140, 143, 147, 157

Case, debate, 113. *See also* Affirmative side and Negative side
Causal reasoning, 101, 103-105, 110
Centimeter-Kilometer, 105-107, 109, 111
Chairperson, responsibilities of, 140-143, 146, 157, 162-170

Changing word order, to make meanings memorable, 40
Chisholm, Shirley, 28
Choosing a topic
   for a debate, 74-76
   for a group discussion, 144-145, 147
   for a speech, 2-3, 11
Chronological pattern of organization, 28, 41
Clemens, Samuel, 60
Committee, 136, 140, 147, 156-157, 161, 166, 173
Comparative advantages case, 114-116, 125-128
Comparisons, to clarify or support an idea, 18, 23-24, 61, 83, 89
"Completely Closed", 153
Consensus, group, 137, 141
Constructive speeches, 120-123, 125-126
Counterplan, a negative strategy, 116, 118, 125, 128
Credibility, 15, 110

Debate, definition and purpose of, 69-70, 79, 124, 134, 172
Debate formats
   Cross-Examination, 121-123, 128
   Feedback, 124, 128
   Historical, 77-79
   Literary, 77, 79
   Traditional, 120-121, 124, 128
   Two-Person, 121, 128
Deductive pattern of organization, 28, 30, 34, 41
Deductive reasoning, 30, 100-101, 110
Defense of the *Status Quo*, a negative strategy, 116-117, 125, 128
Defining terms
   importance of, 81-82, 125, 127
   ways of, 82-83, 89
Defining the controversy, 85-86
Defining the problem, 85, 155
Democratic leadership, 163-165, 170
Demographic factors, 5-8, 11
Derivation of terms, 82, 89
Directing a group discussion, 165-167, 170
Discussion formats
   buzz session, 140, 143, 147, 157
   committee, 136, 140, 147, 156-157, 161, 166, 173

179

forum, 140, 142-143, 147
panel, 140-143, 145, 147, 166
symposium, 140, 142, 145-147, 157, 166

Either-Or, fallacy of, 105, 107, 111
Evaluating
debates, 127-128, 130
discussion groups, 158
discussion leadership, 170
speeches, 63-65
"Ever Emotional", 152
Evidence. *See also* Supportive materials
importance of, 93-94, 110
locating, 94-95
pre-testing and testing, 95, 110, 127
recording, 97-99, 110
using, 95-96, 110, 113, 126
Examples, as a way of clarifying or supporting an idea, 6, 10-11, 18-20, 24, 61, 82, 89, 95
expanded example, 19
hypothetical example, 19
specific example, 18
Extemporaneous method, 37, 41, 124
Eye contact, 49, 55-56, 122-123, 157

Fact, proposition of, 72-73, 77, 79
Fallacies
attacking, 108-111
defined, 105
types (Slovenly Seven), 105-107, 111, 169
False analogy, 105, 107, 111
False cause, 105, 107, 111
Feedback
defined, 59, 64
negative, 60, 62, 64
neutral, 59-60, 64
positive, 60, 62, 64
Forensic Quarterly, The, 94
"Forever Friendly", 152-153
Forum, 140, 142-143, 147

Garagiola, Joe, 10
Generalizing, 96
Gestures, use of, 54-56
"Getting With" an audience, 4-11.
See also Adapting to audiences
Goldwater, Barry, 22

Group discussion
characteristics, 134, 138, 146-147
flaws, 136-138, 146
focus, 140-143, 147
process, 155-159, 164, 167
purposes, 134, 136, 140-143, 146, 163-164, 166, 172
values, 136-137, 146
Group pressure, 138

Hamilton, Alexander, 78
Handling personality conflicts, 165, 168-170
Harris, LaDonna, 28
Hasty generalization, 105, 107, 111
Heckler, Margaret, 28
Holtzman, Elizabeth, 28
Hoover, Jake, 69
Humor, 10-11, 153, 167
Humorous anecdotes, as an introductory strategy, 35, 124, 167

Identification with others, 8, 165
Inconsistent statements, 108
Inductive pattern of organization, 28, 30-31, 34, 41
Inductive reasoning, 30-31, 101-105, 110
causal reasoning, 101, 103-105, 110
reasoning by analogy, 101-103, 110
reasoning by example, 101-102, 110
sign reasoning, 101, 103, 110
Inherent problems, 87, 114-117
Initiating a group discussion, 165-166, 170
Interviews, as source of information, 16, 94, 141, 153

Jefferson, Thomas, 78
Johnson, Davey, 102
Johnson, Lady Bird, 29
"Jolly Joker", 153
Jordan, Barbara, 28
Judging a debate, 127-128

Kelley, Clarence, 17
Kennedy, John F., 40
King, Coretta, 28
King, Martin Luther, Jr., 37

Laissez-faire "leadership", 163-164, 170
Language
   appropriate, 38-39, 41
   clear, 38-41
   memorable, 38, 40-41
   using words orally, 38-41
Laughter, handling of, 60
Leadership
   emerging (A, B, C, D), 161-162, 164, 170
   responsibilities, 140-143, 146, 157, 162-170
   types, 163-165, 170
Lectern, use of, 48-49
Lincoln, Abraham, 36, 78
Listening, improving, 61-62, 64, 153-154
Loaded questions, 23-24
Loaded words, 40, 71
Lombardi, Vince, 107

MacLaine, Shirley, 29
McGovern, George, 22
Metaphor, 40-41
Microphone, use of, 48
Minor repairs case, 116-118, 125, 128
Monroe, Alan, 32
Monroe's Motivated sequence, 32-34
Monthly Catalog of U.S. Government Publications, 94

National Forensic League, 122
National University Extension Association, 94
Needs case, 114-116, 125-128
Negation, as a means of defining terms, 82, 89
Negative side
   defined, 70, 79
   duties of, 82, 113-114, 116
   plan, 88
   speaker responsibilities, 125-126, 128
   strategies, 116-118, 125-126, 128
Newsweek, 22, 99
Nonverbal communication, 46-56, 59
   appearance, 46, 54, 56
   body movement, 47-49, 54-56
   eye contact, 47, 49, 55-56, 122-123, 157
   facial expression, 47, 54-55
   gestures, 54-56
   seating arrangements, 49, 56, 141, 157, 159
   vocal characteristics, 51-54, 56, 62
Note cards, use of, 48

Organizing a speech
   body—organizational patterns
      chronological pattern, 28, 41
      deductive pattern, 28, 30, 34, 41
      inductive pattern, 28, 30-31, 34, 41
      problem-solution pattern, 28-29, 34, 41
      psychological pattern, 28, 32-34, 41
      spatial pattern, 28, 34, 41
      topical pattern, 28-29, 34, 41
   conclusions, 28, 36-37, 41
   introductions, 28, 34-36, 41
Over-identification, 8

Panel, 140-143, 145, 147, 166
Parliamentary procedure, 173
Patronizing statements, 7
Pause, as a rhetorical device, 53, 60
Personal identification as an introductory strategy, 35-36, 41
Phrasing a topic
   for a debate, 70-72, 79, 144
   for discussion, 144-145
Pitch, vocal, 51-53, 60
Planning a group discussion, 165-166, 170
Plato, 69
Policy, proposition of, 72-75, 77-79, 85
Practicing your speech, 45-46, 124-125
Prima facie case, 113-114
Problem-solution pattern of organization, 28-29, 34, 41
Problem-solving, process of group discussion, 155-159
Promoting interaction, 165, 167-170
Proof, defined, 18. *See also* Supportive materials
Proposition, the debate
   compared to affirmative plan, 87
   phrasing, 70-72, 79, 144
   types, 72-74, 77-79
Psychological pattern of organization, 32-34, 41

Quality of the voice, 51-52

Rate, of speech, 53, 60
Readers' Guide to Periodical Literature, 16, 95
Reasoning. *See also* Inductive and Deductive

defined, 100, 110
   testing, 100-105, 108-111, 122, 127
Reasoning by analogy, 101-103, 110
Reasoning by example, 101-102, 110
Rebuttal speeches, 120-122, 126-128
Recording information on note cards, 17-18, 24, 97-99, 145
Redford, Robert, 73
Reference to current events, as an introductory strategy, 35, 41
Reference to a historical event, as an introductory strategy, 35-36, 41
Refutation, 108-111, 117, 120, 125-128
Research (knowing your subject well), 16, 24, 94-95, 141, 145, 147, 152-153, 172
Responsible speaking, 17, 23-24
Rhetorical questions, 35, 41
Robert's Rules of Order, 173
Rockefeller, John D., 3rd, 99
Roles
   in a group discussion, 149-154
   positive, 150-151, 153-154, 159, 162
   small actor roles, 152-153

Scenario, for a discussion, 155, 167
Seating patterns
   adjusting your speech to, 49, 56
   for discussion groups, 141, 157, 159
Shakespeare, William, 10, 77
Sign Reasoning, 101, 103, 110
Size, as it influences group discussion, 157, 159, 163
Slang, use of, 39, 42
Slovenly Seven, the
   Ad Hominem attacks, 105-106, 111, 169
   Begging the Question, 105-106, 111
   Centimeter-Kilometer, 105-107, 109, 111
   Either-Or, 105, 107, 111
   False analogy, 105, 107, 111
   False cause, 105, 107, 111
   Hasty generalization, 105, 107, 111
Social Sciences and Humanities Index, 95
Solzhenitsyn, Aleksandr, 77
Spatial pattern of organization, 28, 34, 41
Specific issues, 88-89
Speech purposes, 1, 3-4, 11, 32, 34, 62, 172
   entertain, 1, 3-4, 32, 34, 172
   inform, 1, 3-4, 32, 34, 172
   persuade, 1, 3-4, 32, 34, 61-62, 172

Stage fright, 46-47, 56
Startling statement, as an introductory strategy, 35, 41
Statistics, using to clarify or support an idea, 18, 23-24, 61, 95, 145
Status quo, 71, 79, 87-89, 113-118, 120, 125, 127
Steinem, Gloria, 29
Stine, Jane, 97
Stereotyping, 7
Stock issues, 86-89
Supportive materials. *See also* Evidence
   Comparisons, 18, 23-24, 61, 95
   Examples, 6, 10-11, 18-20, 24, 61, 82, 89, 95
   Statistics, 18, 23-24, 61, 95, 145
   Testimony, 18, 20-22, 24, 61, 95, 109-110
   Visual Aids, 18, 20, 24, 95
Suspense-building techniques, 11, 35
Syllogism(s), 30, 100-101, 108
Symposium, 140, 142, 145-147, 157, 166

Testimony, used to clarify or support an idea, 18, 20-22, 24, 61, 95, 109-110
Time limitations
   for debate, 120-122, 124
   for discussion, 163-164, 166-167
   for speeches, 11
Topical pattern of organization, 28-29, 34, 41
Total refutation of the affirmative plan, a negative strategy, 116-117, 128
Truman, Harry S, 77

U.S. News & World Report, 22

Value, proposition of, 72-73, 77, 79, 85
Videotape recorder, 63
Visual aids
   rules for using, 20
   to gain attention, clarify and support ideas, 11, 18, 20, 24
Volume, 53, 60
Vonnegut, Kurt, Jr., 77

Wicker, Tom, 22
World Almanac, 76